Militancy in PAKISTAN and AFGHANISTAN

A brief history of causes and effects

Militancy in PAKISTAN and AFGHANISTAN

A brief history of causes and effects

S. V. Salahuddin

PENTAGON PRESS

First Published in 2012

Published by

PENTAGON PRESS
206, Peacock Lane, Shahpur Jat,
New Delhi-110049
Phones: 011-64706243, 26491568
Telefax: 011-26490600
email: rajan@pentagonpress.in
website: www.pentagonpress.in

Cataloging in Publication Data—DK
Courtesy: D.K. Agencies (P) Ltd. <docinfo@dkagencies.com>

Salahuddin, S. V. (Syed Viqar)
Militancy in Pakistan and Afghanistan : a brief history of causes and effects / S.V. Salahuddin.
p. cm.
Includes bibliographical references (p.).

ISBN 9788182746541

1. Afghanistan—History, Military. 2. Afghanistan—Politics and government—20th century. 3. Federally Administered Tribal Areas (Pakistan)—Politics and government. 4. Radicals—Pakistan—Federally Administered Tribal Areas. 5. Religious militants—Pakistan—Federally Administered Tribal Areas. I. Title.

DDC 958.104 23

Printed at Aegean Offset Printers, Greater Noida, U.P.

CONTENTS

Preamble 9

1. **A Historical Perspective** **13**
The Advent of Islam 14
The Nationalist Uprisings 16
The Decline 18
Iran's Dominance over Afghanistan 19
Relations with British India 21
The First Anglo-Afghan War 24
The Beginning of the 'Great Game' 27
The Second Anglo-Afghan War 28

2. **Afghanistan in the Twentieth Century** **32**
Amir Habibullah Khan (1901-1919) 32
The Anglo-Russian Convention 34
Amir Amanullah Khan 35
Amir Nadir Shah 39
Zahir Shah, the last Afghan King 41
President Sardar Daud Khan 44
Border Issues with Pakistan 45
Loya Jirga 48
Daud's Governance 48

President Noor Muhammad Taraki 50
President Hafizullah Amin 51
President Babrak Karmal 52
President Dr. Najibullah 53

3. Soviet Invasion of Afghanistan 56

Taliban—The Holy Warriors 57
Enter Osama bin Laden 59
Launching Attacks on American Assets 61
Al-Qaeda Training Camps in Afghanistan 66
Operation Enduring Freedom 68

4. Afghanistan's Ethnic Conundrum 74

5. Afghanistan Today 82

US Relations with Pakistan 90
The Death of Osama bin Laden 92
Pak-US Marriage 95

6. How Pakistan was Talibanized? 98

Role of the Media 107
Taliban and the Political Parties in Pakistan's Tribal Belt 109
The Mindset of the Pakistani Taliban 110
Talban's Restrictions on Arts in Pakistan 112

7. Militant Groups and their Leaders 114

FATA (Federally Administered Tribal Areas) 115
Militant Groups in FATA 117
Groups of Taliban Forces in FATA 121
Foreign Militant Groups in Pakistan's Tribal Belt 125
Sources of Taliban Funding 127
Opium as Source of Funding 129

8. The Issues in FATA—A historical perspective **132**

FATA at a Glance 134

Literacy 135

Educational Institutes in FATA versus those in the entire Province of Khyber Pukhtunkhwa 135

Opportunities for Earning a Livelihood in FATA 136

9. Is Taliban Losing its Clout? **139**

Can the Taliban Revive again? 144

Taliban's latest move could help Peace Drive 145

10. Attacks on the NATO Supply Line in Pakistan **147**

NATO Strike on Pakistani Military Posts 149

11. America's New Afghan Policy **155**

Drone Attacks 158

12. Afghanistan after 2014 **161**

What can the United States Accept? 164

End Notes 175

Index 180

PREAMBLE

Afghanistan is located at the crossroads of many civilizations. It is the gateway to India as well as to Central Asia. It shares borders with Pakistan, Iran and the Central Asian Republics of Turkmenistan, Uzbekistan and Tajikistan—a volatile mix of nations in a troubled corner of the world. Historically, the country with the most interest in the region is Russia, which views Central Asia as its backyard, and the nations located within it—stepping stones—to the warm waters of the Arabian Sea. In pursuit of that ambition, Russia over the centuries has gradually expanded its realm by conquering the vast lands of the Caucasus and Muslim Central Asia, eventually pausing at the northern borders of the Indian sub-continent and Afghanistan.

This was the beginning of the "Great Game" a term described by the nineteenth-century British Imperialists to describe the British–Russian struggle to acquire hegemony over the lands of Central Asia and Afghanistan. A century later the "game" goes on. The "Great Game" is no longer a sporting event for distant spectators. It has turned deadly and the intensity of violence it produces in the region, now affects the entire globe.[65]

Seven years after Afghanistan's first-ever Presidential election, the increasingly besieged Government of Hamid Karzai has virtually lost credibility at home and abroad. Al-Qaeda has found a new friend in the region—the Tehrik-e-Taliban of Pakistan (TTP)—that has offered them a safe haven in the tribal belt of the country. The government of Pakistan is on the defensive beset by one political crisis after another and in the aftermath of the killing of Osama bin Laden, at Abbotabad. Its military and Intelligence agency, the I.S.I., stands humiliated and accused of supporting the perpetrators of terror. As a result, the strategic partnership with the US is almost in tatters. Afghanistan has replaced Kashmir as the main arena of the still unresolved struggle between Pakistan and India.

The biggest risk the world faces today is the destabilizing of Pakistan, a poor nation of around 180 million people and in possession of over one hundred nuclear warheads. A victory in Afghanistan would amount to nothing, if the price is the loss of Pakistan to extremist forces. Ten years after the US led coalition and the Afghan commanders it supported pushed the leadership of the Taliban and al-Qaeda out of Afghanistan into Pakistan, an insurgency that includes other groups is gaining ground on both the Afghan and Pakistan side of the border. The question now is, whether America can extricate itself honorably from this quagmire that Afghanistan has become for them, or is it fated to repeat history and go the way of other powers who sought to conquer it?

A long-term foreign troop presence in Afghanistan is simply not tenable. There is no more a political solution in Afghanistan alone than there is a military one. Pakistan's strategic goals in Afghanistan, place it at odds with Afghanistan and India as well as with US objectives in the region. The alternative is not to place Pakistan in a revised "axis of evil." It is to pursue a high level diplomatic initiative designed to build a genuine consensus on the goal of achieving Afghan stability by addressing the legitimate sources of Pakistan's insecurity. China, both an ally of Pakistan and potentially the largest investor in both Pakistan and Afghanistan, could play a significant role, as could Saudi Arabia, a serious investor in and ally of Pakistan, former supporter of the Taliban and custodian of Islam's two holiest shrines.

A first step could be the establishment of a contact group on the region, authorized by the UN Security Council.[65] This contact group which would include the five permanent members and perhaps others (NATO, Saudi Arabia), could promote bilateral dialogue between India and Pakistan about their respective interests in Afghanistan and about finding a solution to the Kashmir dispute; seek a long-term political vision for the FATA (Federally Administered Tribal Areas) from the Pakistani government, perhaps one involving integrating the FATA into Pakistan's provinces; involve Moscow in the region's stabilization so that Afghanistan does not become a test of wills between the U.S. and Russia; provide guarantees to Tehran that the US–NATO commitment is not a threat to Iran; and ensure that China's role and interests are brought to bear in international discussions on Afghanistan. Such a dialogue would have to be backed by the pledge of a multi-year international development aid package for regional economic integration, including aid to the most affected regions in Afghanistan, Pakistan and Central Asia.

A central purpose of the contact group would be to assure Pakistan that the international community is committed to its territorial integrity and to help resolve the Afghan and Kashmir border issues so as to better define Pakistan's territory. The international community would have to provide transparent assurances and aid to Pakistan, pledge that no state is interested in its dismemberment and guarantee open borders between Pakistan and both Afghanistan and India. The United States and the European Union would have to open up their markets to Pakistan's critical exports, especially textiles, and to Afghan products. And the US would have to offer a road map to Pakistan to achieve the same kind of nuclear deal as was reached with India.

Reassurances by the contact group that addressed Pakistan's security concerns might encourage Pakistan to promote, rather than hinder an internationally and nationally acceptable settlement in Afghanistan. Pakistan, the largest troop contributor to the UN peacekeeping operations, sees itself as a legitimate international power, rather than a spoiler.

India would also need to become more transparent about its activities in Afghanistan, especially regarding the role of its intelligence agency, the Research Analysis Wing (RAW). Perhaps the ISI and the RAW could be persuaded to enter into a dialogue to explore whether the covert war they have waged against each other for the past 60 years could spare the territory of Afghanistan. The contact group could help establish a permanent Pakistan–Indian body at the intelligence and military levels, where complaints could be lodged and discussed. The World Bank and the Asian Development Bank could also set up joint reconstruction programs in Afghanistan. A series of regional conferences on economic cooperation for the reconstruction of Afghanistan have already created a partial framework for such programs.

Then there is Iran. The Bush administration responded to Iranian cooperation in 2001 by placing Tehran in the "axis of evil" and by promising to keep all options on the table which is understood as a code for not ruling out a military attack. Iran has reacted in part by aiding insurgents in Afghanistan to signal how much damage it could do in response. Some Iranian officials, however, continue to seek cooperation with the United States against al-Qaeda and Taliban. Iran would have to be reassured by the contact group that the Afghan territory would not be used as a staging area for activities meant to undermine Iran and all covert activities of U.S. taking place from there would be stopped.

Russia's main concern—that the United States and NATO are seeking permanent US-NATO military presence in Afghanistan and Central Asia—will also need to assuaged.[71] Russia should be assured that US and NATO forces can help defend, rather than threaten, legitimate Russian interests in Central Asia, including through cooperation with the Shanghai Cooperation Organization. Russia and the Central Asian States should be informed of the results of legitimate interrogations of militants who came from the former Soviet space and were captured in Pakistan or Afghanistan.

The region needs to discover a source of mutual benefit derived from cooperation. China—with its development of mineral resources and access roads in Afghanistan and Pakistan, the financial support it gave to build the port of Gwadar in Pakistan and its expansion of the Karakoram Highway, which links China to northern Pakistan—may be that source. China is also a major supplier of arms and nuclear equipment to Pakistan. China has a major interest in peace and development in the region because it desires a north–south energy and trade corridor so that its goods can travel from Xinjiang to the Arabian Sea ports of Pakistan so that oil and gas pipelines can carry energy from the Persian Gulf and Iran to western China. In return for such a corridor, China could help deliver much-needed electricity to both countries. Such corridor would also help revive the economies of both Afghanistan and Pakistan.

The goal of the US should be to put aside the past, Washington's keenness for "victory" as the solution to all problems, and the United States' reluctance to involve competitors, opponents or enemies in diplomacy. A successful initiative will require exploratory talks and an evolving road map. Today such suggestions may seem naïve or impossible, but without such audacity there is little hope for Afghanistan, Pakistan, or for the region as a whole.[65]

1

A Historical Perspective

Afghanistan is located in the northern hemisphere, 29 to 38 degree latitude and 60 to 75 degree longitude. It covers an area of 700,000 square kilometers and has a population of approximately 30 million.[1] Afghanistan is not its original name. Prior to 1747 it was known as Khorasan and in the ancient Vedic scriptures as well as in the Zoroastrian Avesta, its name was recorded as Aryana. The original Aryans came to Afghanistan from Central Asia and from there spread to India and Europe. It is believed that the major part of *Rig Ved*, the religious book of the Aryans, was composed in Afghanistan. It is also believed that the Zoroastrians began proselytizing in Afghanistan, from where the religion eventually found its way into Persia (Iran).

The Avesta mentions three ancient dynasties of Aryana namely Paradatas, Kowas and Ispas.[2] The founder of the Paradatas dynasty was Yama who ruled Aryana approximately 5000 years ago from his capital Bakhti, while that of the Kowas dynasty was Koikawata who also ruled from Bakhti. The founder of the Ispas dynasty was Lahrapa. Zoroastrianism made its first debut in Aryana during the rule of Lahrapa's son Vashtaspa who was born in approximately 1000 BC in Balkh in the present day Uzbekistan.[5]

Towards the end of the Ispas dynasty, the country had broken up into small fiefdoms. At the time of the invasion of Afghanistan by Alexander the Great, the ruler was a warlord named Bayas. The first province which capitulated to the Greeks was Herat which fell in 329 BC. This was followed by the fall of Arakosia and Kandahar. Alexander laid siege to Kabul and captured it in 328 BC. He built forts in Herat, Sistan, Kandahar and Kabul for use by his troops. It took Alexander four years to consolidate his rule. He then led his troops out of the Khyber Pass into the Indian subcontinent, after appointing several of his generals as governors, of the captured provinces. One of the descendents of these governors set up an independent dynasty in Balkh in 250 BC which lasted for approximately two centuries.[3]

In the third century BC the then ruler of the Morya dynasty in India, captured a large portion of Afghanistan and introduced Buddhism. The most famous ruler of this dynasty was Ashoka (273 to 232 BC) who propagated the Buddhist faith in the region and beyond. After the Morya dynasty, Afghanistan continued to be ruled by Indian princesses. Under these rulers, Buddhism flourished and spread as far as the Sing kiang province of China and Kashgar in Central Asia. During this period, a place called Capia (now known as Bagram) became the summer capital and Peshawar the winter capital of the empire.

The descendents of Ashoka could not hold on to the vast empire and as a result Afghanistan once again split up into small fiefdoms. In the fifth century BC the Huns and the Sassanids fought each other for dominance.[4] The Huns prevailed and gained control of Afghanistan in 460 AD. During their rule they destroyed all vestiges of Buddhism. Their dominance did not last long. The Sassanid of Persia and the Guptas of India eventually succeeded in eliminating the Huns.

The Advent of Islam

Afghanistan was ruled by the Brahman Shahan Dynasty before the arrival of Islam. They were the first dynastic family in Afghanistan's history who made Kabul their capital in 630 AD. The Arabs fired by the zeal of their new religion—Islam—were in the ascendency and stemming their advance became the priority of the Afghan rulers. The Arabs actually moved towards Afghanistan around 640 AD in pursuit of the Persian (Iranian) King Yazdgard who after his defeat took refuge there. The first battle between the Arabs and the Afghans took place in 645 AD and by 654 AD the Arabs had occupied the districts of Marv, Nishapur, Karman and Zaranj.[5] The invaders initially had a difficult time subduing the country.

However, the situation changed, when a number of tribes who had been oppressed by the then ruler Taiful Maluki, changed sides, converted to Islam and became the fighting arm of the Arab army. Despite the positive development, the Arab armies continued to face significant opposition. Thus for example, over a ten year period (645 to 654 AD), the Arabs attacked Kabul six times but were beaten back each time.[8]

As a counter strategy, the Baghdad based Umayad Caliph established an Arab colony, north of Merv in 672 AD, comprising 10,000 families. The Arab influence remained restricted to the districts of Merv and Nishapur while the rest of the country was held firmly by the local warlords. This status quo prevailed for over a century. Neither the Arabs were able to take control of Afghanistan, nor were the warlords able to expel them from the country.

While the Arabs failed militarily, their missionaries and religious scholars succeeded beyond their expectations. For the superstitions riddled tribal society, the egalitarian principles of Islam, which originated from the deserts of Arabia, appealed immensely to the Afghans who converted in droves to the new religion. These war mongering tribes, became loyal soldiers of Islam, bent on spreading the faith to the neighbouring lands.[8]

While the Afghans accepted the religion, they could not accept the bondage of the foreign Arab Caliphs based in distant Baghdad. The first nationalist leader was Abu Muslim Khorasani, who took advantage of the upheaval in Baghdad, due to rivalry between two ruling families, the Abbasids and the Umayyads. Abu Muslim participated in the tussle on the side of the Abbasids. On achieving victory, Abu al Abbas al Saffah, the head of the Abbasids, rewarded Abu Muslim by appointing him as the Governor of Khorasan, as Afghanistan was known at that time. In 754 AD on the death of al Saffah, his brother Mansur became the Caliph in Baghdad who resented and felt threatened by Abu Muslim's popularity. In order to reduce his influence and remove him from his power base in Khorasan, Caliph Mansur offered him the Governorship of Syria. Abu Muslim sensing a trap, refused. The Caliph then lured him to Baghdad and had him killed. The death of Abu Muslim ended the dreams for independence of Khorasan (Afghanistan) but became a catalyst for more rebellions in the country against the Arabs.[7]

THE NATIONALIST UPRISINGS

After the death of Abu Muslim, the independence movement, spread to other parts of the country. Taheri was the first nationalist leader from Herat who took up the banner for independence. In 870 AD, he declared independence for Khorasan (Afghanistan) and made Nishapur his capital.[8] Unfortunately, he did not live long. The independence movement ended with his death in 872 AD. Nishapur was then occupied by the forces of the Saffari family whose leader was Yaqub Sistani.

The Safaris were succeeded by the Samanis who had descended from the Zoroastrian clan of Saman from Balkh (ancient Greek Baktra or Zariaspa), in the Bukhara province of Uzbekistan. The descendents of this dynasty ruled Afghanistan and a large part of Iran for about 120 years. Towards the end of the tenth century, in 963 AD, they were defeated by Alaptagin, who was a Samani slave of Turkish origin. He had been appointed a governor in recognition of his martial prowess. He was ambitious and successfully rebelled against his masters, the Samanis, and founded the Ghaznavi dynasty, which survived for over 200 years (973 AD to 1186 AD).[5] The most well known ruler in this dynasty was Mahmud Ghaznavi (998 AD to 1030 AD), renowned for his extraordinary generalship. He also became notorious in history, for sacking and looting the Hindu temple at Somnath. It is noteworthy, that despite the fact that Mahmud Ghaznavi invaded India 17 times, he never established a permanent presence there and always returned back to Khorasan (Afghanistan).[4] Besides martial skills, Mahmud Ghaznvi is also known for his patronage of scholars and men of learning. Some of the well-known scholars at his court included al Beiruni, Utbi, Farabi and the great poet Firdausi. The famed Iranian epic *Shahnama* was compiled by Firdausi at his court.[4]

The glory of the Ghaznavis did not last. The Seljuk's of Central Asia and the Ghauris of the neighbouring province of Ferozkoh repeatedly attacked and destroyed what was once the great Ghaznavi Empire. In 1151 AD, Allauddin Ghauri burnt and ransacked Ghazni the capital. The Ghauri conquerors originated from a place called Ghaur which is a mountainous district to the east of Herat in Afghanistan. Initially, the Ghauris were vassals of the Ghaznavis. This changed when the Ghauris defeated the Ghaznavis in 1186 and destroyed their power. Besides Afghanistan, the Ghauris also attacked and eventually annexed all of northern India including Assam and Bengal. The Ghauris under Qutbuddin Aibek, founded the Ghauri Islamic Sultanate in India. They eventually lost their moorings in Afghanistan and became an Indian dynasty.

Towards the middle of the eleventh century the Saljuks of the Turkmens occupied Afghanistan. Tughral Baig, the General leading the Saljuk troops established the Saljuk dynasty with Nishapur as his capital. Six years later he expanded his realm by conquering more territory in Afghanistan. He was succeeded by his son Sultan Allauddin Khwarzm who decided to attack the Abbasid Caliph in Baghdad so that he could take on the mantle of the Caliph of Islam, if victorious. In 1218 AD he marched with a large army towards Baghdad and while en-route, he was informed of the attack by the Mongols on his own country. Khwarazm turned back, but was unable to stop the Mongol scourge which within three centuries wiped out the vast Khwarzm Empire.[5] During the rule of the last Khwarzm ruler, Allauddin Muhammad, Afghanistan was again attacked by the Mongols, led by Ghengis Khan, who destroyed the eastern provinces. Thereafter, the Mongols captured not only Afghanistan but also a major part of Central Asia.

Like their other victims, Afghanistan too was not spared the Mongol atrocities. The cultures which had evolved in Herat, Ghazni and Balkh, over the centuries, were destroyed and the country reverted to the 'stone age' with perhaps one positive outcome. Many religious scholars and their families, who survived the Mongol holocaust, fled to India preserving certain aspects of the culture and were responsible for proselytizing and spreading Islam in the sub-continent.

Genghis Khan passed away in 1227 AD but his descendents were equally cruel. His grandsons Kublai Khan and Halagu Khan became notorious for the destruction they unleashed on the vanquished territories. The former is also credited with setting up a dynasty in China whereas the latter became notorious for burning the libraries in Baghdad thus bringing to a halt the progress and growth of the Arab civilization. The debilitating effect of that carnage is visible even today in the ethos of the Arab communities.[8]

After the death of Genghis Khan the vast empire ruled by the Mongols, which included Afghanistan, disintegrated. In Afghanistan, chaos and disunity became rampant until Taimur (the lame) came to power towards the end of the fourteenth century. Taimur was descended from Genghis Khan on his mother's side, and was a Muslim by faith. He was however, no less cruel and ruthless to his co-religionists. He was lame in one foot and hence his alias 'the lame one'. Taimur made Samarkand his capital and annexed vast tracts of Turkistan, Afghanistan, Iran, Central Asia and India into his empire. Taimur's empire at its zenith, stretched from the Caspian Sea to the Sinkiang province in China.[3] Despite the vastness of his empire, his desire to acquire more land was never sated. His preparations to attack China were almost complete when he died suddenly in 1405 AD.

After his death, Taimur's descendents eschewed aggression and adopted a more peaceful way of life. The Taimur Empire, which included Afghanistan as a province, lasted for about a century. Taimur was succeeded by his son Shah Rukh in 1405 AD. He was committed to peace and opposed violence and aggression. His wife Gohar Shad Agha was a wise and a talented woman. In addition to providing support to her husband, she also worked at various projects for the benefit of the populace. She also promoted education by setting up schools and higher learning centres throughout the realm. Besides a good administrator, she was also a good ambassador for her nation. Unlike Taimur, Shah Rukh and his wife promoted good ties with China. On the death of Shah Rukh in 1447 AD his only son Ulug Baig became the king. He was perhaps even more enlightened than his father and is credited with the spread of education and particularly the science of astrology throughout his realm which included Afghanistan.[5]

Bilkhaira was the last king of the Taimur dynasty. His rule was a bright epoch in Afghan history. He was fortunate in having a talented prime minister in Amir Ali Shernawai. The King was patron of architecture and his style was copied by the Mughals of India and the Safavis of Iran. The famous architect, Behzad, was born in 1510 during the rule of Bilkhaira. He was later taken away to Iran and appointed the Dean of the Art Library in Tabriz, by the Iranian King Shah Ismail Safavi. The famous poet Abdur Rehman Jami also lived during the rule of Bilkhaira.

The Decline

The sixteenth and seventeenth centuries are regarded as the bleak years of Afghanistan's history.[8] This period impacted negatively on the country's culture and its way of life. In contrast to the glory and richness of culture in the earlier years, the new culture was steeped in superstitions, meaningless rituals, tribalism and ethnicity. The factors that precipitated the fall are described in the following events:

1. Mongol Invasion

The Mongol invasion in 1218 AD was a serious blow to the Afghan culture and way of life. The massacres of the population combined with rape, plunder and loot which the Mongols unleashed on the nation destroyed the centuries old cultural traditions. The barbarity of the Mongols was so vicious that the Afghan society has not recovered even to this day.[4]

2. The Disappearance of Central Government

Towards the end of the Taimur dynasty in 1405 AD the role of a central government became blurred.[8] The link between the ruler and the populace was broken. In its place small principalities with their own chieftains/ warlords evolved. The infighting brought on a sense of hopelessness and despondency in the general population. In these conditions, a tug of war ensued between the neighbouring empires of India and Iran, for control of this unfortunate country. That situation prevails even today with India, Pakistan and Iran vying for control of Afghanistan.

3. New Trade Route

The third reason for the decline was the establishment of a sea route between East and the West.[11] This reduced the importance and usefulness of the silk trade route which passed through Afghanistan. Although this development seems of minor importance, it nevertheless, had a far reaching impact on the future of Afghanistan. It not only lost a significant quantum of tax revenue but the country also became isolated from both the East and the West. Being cut off from the West meant isolation from the latest developments in science and industrial technology in Europe. As a result, Afghanistan got marooned from the rest of the world and descended into poverty and ignorance.

Iran's Dominance over Afghanistan

The ethnic and inter-tribal conflicts further exacerbated the situation. Towards the beginning of the eighteenth century, a large portion of Afghanistan was occupied by the Safavi kings of Iran. The power of the

Safavis declined by the beginning of the eighteenth century[11] loosening their hold on Afghanistan, precipitating a struggle for independence. The rebellion started in the Kandahar province when a notable tribal chieftain Mir Owais Khan killed the Iranian Governor in 1708 AD and established an independent principality. He refused to call himself King and preferred the title of 'Sardar' (chieftain of tribe). On his death Sardar Owais Khan was succeeded by his brother who preferred closer ties with Iran. This was resented by Owais Khan's son Mehmud who deposed his uncle in 1712 AD.

Mehmud proved to be a strong leader. He had a deep grudge against Iran and in 1722 AD, defeated the Iranians at Ispahan. Unfortunately his attack on Iran turned out to be a mistake as instead of consolidating his rule in Kandahar and addressing the issues bedeviling Afghanistan, he chose to attack an enemy thousands of miles away. Although he was able to defeat the Safavis, he did not really benefit from the victory. He also made the mistake of shifting his capital from Kandhar to Ispahan, thus isolating himself from his home territory. In the midst of a strange place and stranger people, he had no choice but to delegate the day-to-day administration of the conquered territory to the Iranians. Thus Mehmud gradually lost control. By conquering Iran, Mehmud had also become a threat to the Russians in the north and the Turks in the west.[11] The wars with these neighbours now became inevitable. In addition, the Iranians proved difficult subjects as they were reluctant to accept the Afghans as their rulers, who they considered culturally inferior.[13]

As a result, a number of rebellions began in Iran against the Afghan rule. Nadir Shah, the Chieftain of the Afshar tribe, finally succeeded with the help of the nationalist tribes in expelling the Afghans. In 1730 AD, after a number of skirmishes, he pushed the Afghans out of Iran and then went on to attack Afghanistan, conquering one province after another until by 1738 AD he had subdued the whole country.[8] After conquering Afghanistan, he marched on to India, through the Khyber Pass, and defeated the Indian Mughal ruler at Karnal. He entered Delhi in triumph on 12 March 1739, and carried out a massacre to rival any Mongol. [11] He looted the treasury and carried back with him the famous peacock throne of the Mughals. He was however, not destined to live long. On reaching Meshed in Iran, he was assassinated in 1747 by his own officers.

After Nadir Shah's death, Iran's occupied territories in Afghanistan once again broke up into small principalities. The Afghan troops serving with

Iran's army, returned back to Afghanistan under the command of Noor Muhammad Ghilzai and Ahmed Khan Abdali. To counter future aggressions from Iran, and to select a new leader, a *jirga* (court of elders) was called in 1747.[12] The debate that ensued lasted for over eight days. Finally, a venerated elder proposed the name of Ahmed Shah Abdali as the next King of Afghanistan. Abdali then, had just turned 25 years old. The young Abdali proved to be a wise choice and in the years to come justified the confidence reposed in him. He worked hard to restore the respect and honor of his nation.

RELATIONS WITH BRITISH INDIA

Abdali was an accomplished general and won every battle that he took part in. His most famous battle was with the Marhattas of India, who wanted to establish Hindu rule in Delhi. Abdali met the Marhatta troops in a battle at Panipat near Delhi and inflicted a crushing defeat, thus saving the Mughal rulers of the day. Abdali could have occupied Delhi, and become the ruler, but instead chose to return back to Afghanistan.[13] For his many contributions to the Afghan cause he is remembered as the father of the nation.

Ahmed Shah Abdali, was succeeded by his son Taimur Shah who could not hold a candle to his father. As a result, Afghanistan once again broke up into small fiefdoms. Fearing for his life, Taimur Shah moved the capital from Kandahar to Kabul where he died in 1793 AD. On his death, conflict broke out between his sons, which ended when his fifth son, Shah Zaman, with the help of the powerful chieftain of the Barakzai tribe, Sardar Painda Khan, captured the throne. Shah Zaman like his grandfather, Ahmed Shah Abdali, was a brave and wise ruler. Unfortunately, due to poor governance by his inept father, he inherited assorted internal and external problems and had to struggle to gain control. Once he had consolidated his power, he decided to expand his realm into India. The British in India were alarmed as they had received reports that Napoleon too was planning an attack on India.[15] To counter the immediate danger, the British Governor General dispatched Captain John Malcolm to the King of Iran, Fateh Ali Shah Qajjar, seeking his help to dissuade the Afghans from advancing towards India. The Iranian King was a British ally and decided to use Shah Zaman's step brother Mehmud, who had taken refuge in his court. Mehmud had been one of the aspirants to the throne of Afghanistan and saw this as an opportune moment to attack Kandahar, with the help of the Iranian King. He succeeded in subduing Kandahar and then turned his attention to Kabul. Shah Zaman at that time was camped at Lahore in India. On hearing of Mehmud's attack, he immediately returned to Afghanistan. But it was too late. Mehmud after the capture of Kandahar and Kabul, declared himself King, and bribed the local sardars to gain their support. Shah Zaman stopped on the way back at the fort of a local chieftain near Jalalabad, who contrary to the traditions of Afghan hospitality, arrested Shah Zaman and handed him over to his step brother. At his orders, Shah Zaman was rendered blind and jailed, where he remained till the end of Mehmud's rule in 1803.

Mehmud proved to be a fickle and inept ruler. He was not interested in the welfare of his people. Soon rebellions broke out throughout the country and the army was unable to control the situation. Encouraged by the turmoil, Shuja ul Mulk who was the real brother of Shah Zaman (from the same mother) attacked Kabul and defeated Mehmud who sued for peace. Shuja arrested him and confined him to the same prison where Shah Zaman had been interned.

Unfortunately, the prevailing political climate was not conducive to peace and stability in the country. The governors of distant provinces aspired to become independent of the central government. The biggest threat to Shah Shuja was from the Prime Minister Fateh Khan who was loyal to ex-King Mehmud. Despite his best efforts, Shuja was unable to tame him or obtain the support of his tribe, the Barakzais. Besides trouble at home, Shuja had to reckon with external threats emanating from Indian Sikhs on the eastern border and from Iran on the west.

The French Emperor Napoleon, at the time, was at the height of his power and in 1807 had signed a friendship treaty with Alexander the First of Russia. Britain was most concerned with this development, and to protect their flanks thought it necessary to offer a friendship treaty to both Afghanistan and Iran.[16] Consequently, a British delegation under General Elphinstone was sent to Afghanistan. Shah Shuja personally received the delegation at Peshawar. A friendship agreement between Afghanistan and the East India Company was signed in 1809. The agreement did not last. Only a few weeks later, the Prime Minister, Fateh khan, defeated Shah Shuja and restored Mehmud to the throne. Shah Shuja took refuge in India, at a place called Ludhiana, where he was pensioned off by the British.

Mehmud had occupied the Afghan throne twice, both times with the help of the Barakzai Sardar, Fateh Khan. So while Mehmud was called the Amir (king), he ruled in name only. The real ruler was Fateh Khan. The King and his oldest son Kamran were unhappy at this arrangement and at the first opportunity arrested Fateh Khan, blinded and imprisoned him. Fateh Khan's brothers, offended by the treatment meted out to their brother, rebelled against the King. He in turn asked his imprisoned former Prime Minister, Fateh Khan to intercede with his bothers, to call off the rebellion. On his refusal the King put Fateh Khan to death. A younger brother of Fateh Khan then attacked Kabul (1820) and defeated Shah Mehmud who along with his son escaped to Herat. Thus ended the Durrani dynasty which is referred to as the as the first Pashtun dynasty in Afghan history. All previous rulers so far had been Farsi (Persian) speaking.

Dost Muhammad Khan is referred to as the founder of the Muhammad Zai Dynasty. He too was a Pashtun. After the end of the Durrani Dynasty, a state of instability existed for almost a quarter of the century. Despite occupying Kabul, the country's capital, Dost Muhammad Khan was not in a position to call himself the ruler of all Afghanistan.[13] But eventually, in 1826, he captured Ghazni and Jalalabad and then marched on to Peshawar to free it from the clutches of the Sikhs of India. He was not successful and eventually had to seek British help.

In the meantime, Muhammad Shah Qajjar, the King of Iran attacked Herat in 1837. Russia supported Iran which alarmed the British. To keep the Russians away from the borders of India, the British decided to seek a friendship pact with the rulers of Herat, Kandahar, Kabul, Sind and Punjab. For this purpose they first sent a delegation headed by Captain Alexander Burns to Kabul. Dost Muhammad Khan saw this as a good opportunity to ask the British to evict the Sikhs from Peshawar as a quid pro quo. The British however, had their hands full and were not willing to take on the Sikhs at this time. While the negotiations dragged on, the Russians sent their own delegation headed by Sergei Vikovich to the Afghan court. The British Governor General in India saw the visit as a treacherous act of double dealing by the Afghans and used it as an excuse to initiate military operations.[17]

The First Anglo-Afghan War

The military conflict which ensued lasted for four years (1838 to 1842) and is recorded in history as the first Anglo-Afghan war. The British succeeded in capturing, Ghazni, Kandahar and Kabul and Dost Muhammad escaped to Bukhara in Central Asia. The British then brought back Shah Shuja, who was living in exile in India, and installed him as a puppet King. Despite regaining his throne, Shah Shuja could not reign. He was unpopular on two counts. First he had regained his throne with the help of an external power, and secondly he was seen as a puppet in the hands of the British. In the eyes of the Afghans, by installing a puppet king, the British had successfully extended their colonization from India to Afghanistan.[17]

The Afghan people rose en masse against their ruler and his British minders. For the British this was a new experience. They were not fighting against a regular army but the entire Afghan nation, who driven by a nationalist fervor, had risen to evict the foreign invader. Seeing that the public sentiment had turned in his favour, Dost Muhammad Khan returned from his Central Asian exile to Afghanistan and with the help of the nationalists, reoccupied his throne. In a battle near Kabul, the British forces under General Seal, suffered a crushing defeat by the nationalist troops. While the victory was significant, the euphoria did not last. The British forces in Kabul eventually regained control and took Dost Muhammad prisoner and sent him and his family in exile to India.[18]

In the absence of Dost Muhammad Khan, his son Akbar Khan took up the cudgels. The constant skirmishes with the nationalist forces and the harsh winter finally forced the British to reach a compromise with Akbar Khan and prepared to return to India. In January 1842, the approximately sixteen thousand British troops in Kabul, began their march back. On the way they were ambushed by militants, who had taken positions on the surrounding hills and a massacre ensued. Out of the sixteen thousand troops, only one soldier limped back to India to tell his tale.[18] The British military expedition had failed miserably. Their puppet ruler Shuja Shah was also killed by his nationalist compatriots. The British, in order to diffuse tensions and to protect their flanks on the western border, released Dost Muhammad Khan and allowed him to return to Afghanistan.

Dost Muhammad's received a royal welcome on his return home. In his absence, his son Akbar Khan, acting on his behalf, had negotiated ably with the local warlords to smoothen the differences. Dost Muhammad was pleased with the welcome and appointed his son as the Prime Minister and heir apparent. However, the father and son soon fell apart on issues relating to foreign affairs. The young and impetuous Akbar Khan wanted an aggressive policy on the pattern of Ahmed Shah Abdali. The father on the other hand wanted a balanced and measured approach to the external problems facing the country. Failing to get his father's support, the son headed to Herat where his father-in-law was the Sardar. He also made plans to seek help from the Qajjar King of Iran. The potential clash between father and son was averted by the untimely death of Akbar Khan. Dost Muhammad then appointed his second son as the prime minister and heir apparent.

The Sikhs, in the past, had cast their lot with the British against Dost Muhammad Khan. But, all that changed after the first war between the Sikhs and the British (1845 to 1846) when the Sikhs recognizing the danger the British posed for them joined hands with Dost Muhammad and gifted Peshawar to him in 1848, to cement the relationship.[18]

The Second Anglo-Sikh war was fought in 1848-49. The Afghans contributed a cavalry brigade as part of the friendship agreement with the Sikhs. The brigade however could not participate in the battle as the Sikhs lost the skirmish before the Afghans could join them. The victorious British annexed all territory which had been in Sikh possession, which included the city of Peshawar, recently gifted to the Afghans.[19]

In the 12 year period between 1843 and 1855 there were minimal contacts and a cold war prevailed between the British and the Afghans. After 1855 the relations between Afghanistan and British India improved, primarily because of deteriorating relations between Britain and Iran. In 1855 an agreement was signed between Ghulam Haider Khan, the son of Dost Muhammad Khan, and the Chief Commissioner of Punjab Sir John Lawrence in Peshawar. Under the terms of this agreement it was agreed:[21]

1. the signatories shall preserve peace and promote friendship between the two countries and shall respect the territorial integrity and boundaries of the two countries.
2. the enemies of the British shall be considered the enemies of the Amir (King) of Afghanistan and the friends of the British shall be the friends of the Amir

With this agreement, the cold war between the two countries was brought to an end. In 1855, a sardar named Muhammad Yusuf occupied Heart, by dispossessing the incumbent Sardar Syed Muhammad Khan who in turn asked the King of Iran for help. The Iranian King acceded to the request and sent his troops to Herat. The British in India took note of the growing influence of Iran in Afghanistan and decided to sign a fresh agreement with Afghanistan with the following amendments in the previous agreement:

1. In order to secure Afghan borders, the Government of British India would pay the Amir one hundred thousand rupees per month.
2. To ensure compliance of the terms, a team of British officers will be stationed in Afghanistan. This team however, shall not interfere in the affairs of the country. On completion of the term of the agreement, the team shall return to India.
3. There will be an exchange of ambassadors. The British ambassador shall be posted in Kabul, and the Afghan ambassador will be posted in Peshawar.

In the meantime the Iranian troops had arrived in Herat and removed Muhammad Yusuf and handed back the province to the aggrieved Sardar Muhammad Khan. The tug of war between Britain and Iran, for dominance in Afghanistan, continued until 1857 when a settlement was reached in Paris defining the limits of authority for the two adversaries.[19]

In 1853, after the death of his second son and heir apparent Ghulam Haider Khan, Dost Muhammad Khan appointed his third son Sher Ali Khan as the new heir apparent. In 1863, on the death of his father, Sher Ali declared himself the new Amir of Afghanistan. As mentioned earlier, after the first Afghan-Anglo war (1838 to 1842) there was minimal contact between the British and the Afghans for over 12 years. In that period the British forces had occupied the provinces of Sind and Punjab in India. Their occupied territory now extended to the frontier of Afghanistan. Apparently, after this latest acquisition, there was a limited scope for further expansion. However, in 1865, the British Government in London forwarded to its Government in India, a document written by Sir Henry Rawlinson of its East India Company office in which it was proposed that:[17]

1. Afghanistan be brought into the British sphere of influence as a protectorate.

2. Steps be taken to strengthen the image of Britain in Kabul, and bring it at par with the standing of British emissary Captain Alexander Burns, in the court of Dost Muhammad Khan in 1837.
3. To ensure security in areas adjoining Afghanistan, the Afghan city of Quetta shall be brought under British control, by force if necessary, and army check posts set up in the areas around it.

All these recommendations were in conflict with Lord Lawrence's (British India's Viceroy) policy of neutrality and non-interference in Afghan affairs. Consequently the Government of India did not show much enthusiasm for the Rawlinson's proposals and on 4 February 1879, the Indian Government responded that "in the present circumstances, interference in the internal matters of Afghanistan, appointment of a British Resident in Kabul and stationing of a contingent of British troops, and occupying of territory in the Amir's realm, will lead to hatred in the Afghan population". In addition, the Viceroy was concerned with the growing threat of Russia, and the exorbitant cost involved in implementing the proposal and recommended that it be shelved for the time being.[19]

THE BEGINNING OF THE 'GREAT GAME'

It may be noted that until early nineteenth century, there were no real clash of interests between Russia and Britain in the region. The Russian border, after all, was still 1400 miles away. The situation changed quickly by the middle of the century when Russia moved to occupy vast tracts of land in Central Asia. Its borders now touched the northern borders of India.[21]

The Russian expansion began in 1839 when Count Perovski a Russian General, attacked Khiva in Uzbekistan but had to terminate the expedition due to shortage of food and inclement weather. Like the British army, who suffered horrendous losses while retreating from Kabul, the Russian army also suffered similar deprivations retreating from Khiva. Both expeditions coincidently took place in the same year (1839).[21] Despite the debacle, the Russians returned and soon occupied territory right up to the Syr Darya (river) in Uzbekistan. The Russian expansion was temporarily halted by the Crimean War. At the end of the war, the Russian expansion in Central Asia resumed and soon all Khanates which included Kazakhstan, Kyrgyzstan, Uzbekistan and Turkmenistan were occupied, bringing the Russian frontier to the Afghan and Indian borders by 1866.

The Amir of Afghanistan was perturbed by this development and believed that a friendship treaty with one of the two powers on his borders, namely Britain or Russia, could ensure freedom and independence for his nation.[21] The Amir, Sher Ali, was also concerned that his nephew, Abdur Rehman Khan who was at that time living in Tashkent, was susceptible to Russian influence and could become a threat to him. It was in this frame of mind that he turned to the British for protection.[21] At the invitation of Lord Mayo, the Viceroy of India, Sher Ali went to India in 1869. He received a warm welcome which was very reassuring to him. At the meeting, he sought an agreement with the British on the following parameters:[22]

1. British India shall come to the aid of Afghanistan in the event of an attack by the Russians.
2. The 1853 agreement with British India should be reviewed, as it was one sided. The clauses should be revised to make them more equitable from Afghan perspective.
3. The Government of India should accept the Amir's favourite son Abdullah Jan as heir apparent instead of his eldest son

The viceroy, however, was non-committal on all these points and reluctant to conclude an agreement. Instead, a diplomatic communiqué was issued in which it was stated:

1. The Amir's apprehension regarding aggression by the Russians was without foundation.
2. The Government of India had no intentions of interfering in Afghanistan's internal matters.
3. The Government of India would consider any intrigue against the Amir by his opponents with disfavour. In the event of such development, the Government shall take necessary steps to ensure that the Amir continues to rule with justice and fairness and is able to transfer his rights to his lawful descendents.
4. The Amir was bound under the agreement to keep the Government of India informed on all matters of mutual interest.

THE SECOND ANGLO-AFGHAN WAR

In 1873, Russia carried out extensive military exercises on the border with

Afghanistan. The Amir was alarmed and immediately sent his emissary to India to meet the Viceroy Lord Northbrook. The Viceroy sympathized with the Afghans and sought permission from the Prime Minister in London for signing a defense pact. London was not agreeable and consequently the Amir was informed that the internal problems of Afghanistan were no concern of the British Indian Government.[22]

A change of Government soon took place in Britain, whereby Disraeli and Lord Salisbury became the Prime Minister and Secretary India office respectively. Both were strong proponents of Sir Henry Rawlinson's 'Forward Policy Plan,' under which Afghanistan like India would become a protectorate of Britain. To put this plan into action, the new Government in 1872 appointed a diehard proponent of the 'Forward Policy Plan', Lord Lytton, as the new Viceroy of India. Lord Lytton immediately put pressure on the Amir to accept the appointment of a British Resident in Kabul. The Amir refused.

During this period, the Crimean war which lasted a year (1877 to 1878) broke out. Britain sided with Turkey against Russia.[23] The war which was fought in Europe had worldwide repercussions, especially in Central and South East Asia. In Britain there were fears that Russia would once again test the frontiers of India. This was unacceptable to the British who preferred that any battle with the Russians be fought on the Afghan soil and not on Indian.[21]

In preparation for a potential conflict with Russia, Britain signed an agreement with the Khan of Kalat, a state in Baluchistan, under which the city of Quetta would come under British control. The city is located on the border with Afghanistan, and provides passage for troops into Afghanistan through Kandahar if needed. The Amir of Afghanistan was well aware of the danger that Britain now posed for his independence.[23] Both Britain and Russia were keen on posting their respective ambassadors in Kabul. The Amir was mindful of the fact that his nephew Abdur Rehman Khan, who was a strong aspirant to his throne, was presently living in Tashkent in the pay of the Russians.[24] As Britain was not willing to sign a defense pact with Afghanistan, the Amir feared that the Russians could march in, any day, and install his nephew in his place. Also, on 13 July 1878, a peace agreement was signed between Russia and Britain in Berlin, Germany,[24] under which Russia declared its disinterest in Afghanistan's affairs. On the other hand, Britain was keen to establish its presence in Kabul and on 14 August 1878 the Viceroy Lord Lytton, wrote to the Amir asking him to receive a British delegation in Kabul. It was a coincidence that the Amir's favourite son Abdullah Jan died on 17 August 1878 and he was preoccupied, so did not respond to the Viceroy. Without waiting any longer for the Amir's response, a delegation under Sir Neville Chamberlain was dispatched to Kabul. The Commander of the Afghan Border Guards at Jamrud refused them entry. The Viceroy was infuriated and on 21 November 1878 declared war on Afghanistan.

The British troops entered Afghanistan through three passes namely Khyber, Bolan and Kurram. The battle took place near Kabul and the Afghans, who were unable to stand against the superior British forces, scattered. The British occupied Kabul and installed Sher Ali's son Yaqub Khan as the new Amir. Sher Ali died a broken man on 21 February 1879. The British also forced the new Amir to accept harsh terms of surrender and on 18 March 1879 an agreement known as the Gundmuk accord was signed, under which: [24]

1. Afghanistan would surrender the Khyber and Kurram passes as well as a vast tract of land on which the cities of Sibi, Pishin and Loralai were located.
2. The Amir gave an undertaking that he would not join in any intrigue with the Russians against the British.
3. A British Resident, Sir John Cavagnari, was appointed to the court of the Amir.
4. The foreign policy of Afghanistan would henceforth be determined by the Government of British India.
5. In the event of an attack on Afghanistan, the Government of India would come to its defense.

On the face of it, life returned to normal after the signing of the Gundmuk agreement. But, behind the peaceful façade, the Afghan sardars and warlords seethed with anger at the abject surrender. Consequently, as soon as the British Indian troops returned home, the nationalists attacked the British Residency on 3 September 1879.[24] The British Resident, Sir Louis Cavagnari, along with his entire staff was killed. On receiving the news, the viceroy immediately dispatched 40,000 troops under General Roberts to crush the rebellion. The General occupied Kabul and imposed martial law in the country. An investigation was conducted and the guilty sardars and chieftains were hanged. Yaqub khan placed himself at the mercy of the British. He was arrested and exiled to Calcutta. In the meantime, the Government expressing displeasure at the policies pursued by Lord Lytton, recalled him to London. He was replaced by Lord Ripon who favoured a policy of non-interference in Afghan affairs and accordingly withdrew all British Indian troops from Afghanistan. The war of succession ended with Sher Ali Khan's nephew, Abdur Rahman Khan of Tashkent, becoming the new Amir.[24]

Abdur Rahman had spent many years in exile in Russian controlled Tashkent and Samarkand, due to enmity with his Uncle. He appeared on the scene for the first time, during the second Anglo-Afghan War in 1878 and manoeuvered successfully to become the Amir. Lord Lytton, the Viceroy welcomed him to the throne and signed a friendship agreement in 1880, which is known as the Kabul Treaty. Under this treaty:

1. All British personnel serving in Kabul were to be recalled to India. The position of Resident would not be filled.
2. Amir Abdur Rahman Khan would henceforth receive a yearly stipend of Rupees 1,200,000.
3. There would be no interference in the Afghanistan's internal affairs and in the event of outside aggression, its defense was guaranteed by the British Government in India.

Despite the improvement in relations with the British, Amir Abdur Rahman had to contend with a number of internal problems. The tensions with the British had badly affected the authority of the central government. The sardars and warlords had set up their own fiefdoms, and no longer feared the government in Kabul, creating a poor law and order situation. This then became the Amir's first priority. He succeeded in his efforts to a very large extent and peace once again returned to Afghanistan. Amir Abdur Rahman died in 1901 and was succeeded by his son Amir Habibullah Khan.

2

AFGHANISTAN IN THE TWENTIETH CENTURY

AMIR HABIBULLAH KHAN (1901-1919)

Amir Abdur Rahman Khan had anointed his eldest son as heir apparent in his lifetime. Thus, after his death, on 3 October 1901, Habibullah Khan was crowned Amir of Afghanistan. His rule is considered the beginning of the modernization of the Afghan society. Habibullah Khan was a farsighted ruler,[25] who implemented a number of projects to move the Afghan society forward. For example, in 1903, he set up a college for advanced studies, which was named 'Habibia'. The graduates of this college made significant contributions to the promotion of education and culture in the country for many years. He introduced many of the latest developments in the field of media communication and in 1903 a weekly newspaper called *Siraj ul Akhbar* was published for the first time in the country.[26]

Habibullah, during the 18 years of his rule, had to continuously grapple with challenges from Russia and Britain. Internally, however, he had smooth sailing. The credit for that can be given to the reforms initiated by his father. Lord Curzon, the British Viceroy in India, expressed his unhappiness with the agreement signed with his father, Amir Abdur Rahman, and wanted the new Amir to sign a fresh agreement taking into account the changed circumstances following the second Anglo-Afghan war in 1878. Failing to get a satisfactory response, the Government of India started putting pressure. The British commanders on the Indian-Afghan frontier stopped transit movement of all military equipment and other goods across the border. When the Amir protested, the Viceroy replied that the only way out was for the Amir to come to India and sign a new agreement. The Amir continued to hold out and finally Lord Curzon sent a formal invitation inviting him for discussions. When this did not elicit a response, in desperation, the Viceroy asked the Government in London to permit him to take military action against the Afghans.[25] The permission was denied and Lord Curzon was advised not to jeopardize peace in the region. For a while a state of uncertainty prevailed but thereafter, the Viceroy Lord Curzon, returned home to England on a long leave of absence. In 1904, the Acting Viceroy Baron Ampthill, dispatched a delegation to Kabul[26] under Sir Louis Dean. The delegation remained there from December 1904 to 29 March 1905 during which the following proposals were discussed:[27]

1. A railway line to be installed between Peshawar and Kabul and between Kabul and Chaman near Quetta. Also, a telegraphic line to be installed connecting the two countries.
2. In return, all military equipment for Afghan use to be imported exclusively by way of India.

The Amir rejected clause 2 as it violated the sovereign rights of his country. He also refused to sign a fresh agreement as he did not see any reason why the agreement which his father Amir Abdur Rahman Khan had signed with the British was no longer valid. In response the British threatened to withdraw their ambassador from the country and break all diplomatic ties. The threat had no affect and after protracted negotiations, both parties agreed on a revised draft under which, Amir Habibullah Khan was recognized as a sovereign King of Afghanistan and in recognition of his independent status, he would henceforth be addressed as 'His Majesty' and not as 'His Highness'.

With this impediment out of the way, and at the invitation of the Viceroy Lord Minto, Amir Habibullah Khan toured India for a month beginning on 2 January 1907. He was greeted with a 21-gun salute and a letter from King Edward VII welcoming the Amir. The Amir stayed until 7 March 1907 during which he visited various places of interest which included the Muslim College at Aligarh, in the U.P. province, and Lahore, the capital of the Punjab province, where he laid the foundation of the Islamia College. He also donated twenty thousand rupees for the construction of the building.

THE ANGLO-RUSSIAN CONVENTION

In 1908, Britain and Russia signed an agreement, which came to be known as the Anglo-Russian Convention. In addition to other peripheral issues, Afghanistan came up for special mention. Russia was assured that Britain had no intention of interfering in Afghan affairs or to occupy any part of Afghan territory. Russia too declared that they considered Afghanistan out of their sphere of influence. In the last clause of the agreement it was acknowledged, that while the Amir of Afghanistan was not a party to the agreement, nevertheless, as a courtesy he would be briefed on the contents.

The Amir however, termed it a "cloak and dagger agreement."[28] In his opinion the agreement violated the sovereignty and independence of the Afghan nation. The Viceroy tried to convince the Amir otherwise and reiterated Britain's resolve to guarantee the independence of Afghanistan. But, it was to no avail. The Amir remained adamant and refused to endorse the agreement. In the meantime, the First World War broke out in 1914. Amir Habibullah Khan shrewdly decided to stay neutral.[29] This was not an easy endeavour especially when the entire world was embroiled, directly or indirectly, in the conflagration. The Amir was put in a tight spot especially, when Turkey sided with Germany in the war. The Turkish Sultan was also the Caliph of the Muslim world and his word and actions were considered sacrosanct.[30] A delegation comprising Germans and Turks headed by Kazim Bey of Turkey arrived in Kabul to pressurize the Amir. The Amir would not give in and finally the delegation left Kabul empty handed.

The policy of neutrality adopted by Amir Habibullah Khan was also in the interest of Britain. Any tilt towards the Germans could have created innumerable problems for the British in India. Britain expressed its appreciation and in September 1915, King George VI wrote to the Amir and thanked him.[31] The Amir reassured the British King of his resolve to stay neutral. He also wrote on similar lines to the Viceroy of India.

While the Amir received accolades from Britain, internally, he was reviled by the nationalists. It was generally believed that there was a secret understanding between the Amir and the British, that as a reward for remaining neutral, the British would protect the Amir in the event of a rebellion by nationalist forces. On 29 February 1919 the Amir was assassinated at his hunting lodge in the Luqman Valley. The assassination was blamed on the nationalists who were angry with Amir's obsequious loyalty to the British.

History would record that Amir Habibullah was an enlightened ruler who initiated many reforms for the welfare of his people.[32] He was not a ruthless leader and treated the tribes with respect and consideration. He declared general amnesty for the tribal leaders who were exiled by his father and invited them back to Afghanistan.

AMIR AMANULLAH KHAN

After the assassination of Amir Habibullah Khan, his younger brother Sardar Nasrullah Khan declared himself the Amir. The declaration was supported by Amir Habibullah's eldest son Sardar Inayat ullah Khan. Amir Habibullah's younger son, Sardar Amanullah Khan, however, did not accept the new arrangement. He had been in control of the treasury as well as the bulk of the army under his father's rule. Sardar Nasrullah Khan realized his own vulnerability and agreed to step down in favour of his younger nephew. Nonetheless, on becoming King, Amanullah had his Uncle arrested on charges of conspiring to kill his father, and imprisoned him for life. He also declared that Afghanistan was independent in making decisions pertaining to all external or internal matters.

To ensure that his declaration of independence had registered with the British, he sent a copy of it to the Viceroy, voicing the hope that the Government of India would respect it.[31] When a response was not forthcoming, Amanullah began stationing troops on the border with India. The British retaliated with a buildup on their side of the border. Although the Afghan troops were fewer in number and less equipped, they were able to push back the Indian troops in the skirmishes that followed. The Afghans also succeeded in occupying a British picket on the Peshawar-Bannu road. In another skirmish, the Afghans forced a British battalion to retreat forty miles from the border.

The tribal leaders were greatly emboldened by this 'victory' and attacked the British positions from different directions, using guerilla tactics. As a result, a large number of Indian troops absconded from the front. The British finally realized that the Afghan nationalists were a force to be reckoned with and on 20 July 1919 agreed to a truce and concluded a treaty on the following terms:[33]

(i) The external policy of Afghanistan will not be subject to controls by the Government of India.

(ii) The Governments of Afghanistan and Britain shall appoint their ambassadors in London and Kabul respectively. Afghanistan will be free to appoint its ambassadors in the countries of its choice around the world.

(iii) The status of Afghanistan would be that of a free and an independent nation. The Amir shall henceforth be addressed as 'His Majesty' and accorded respect due to a reigning monarch.

Following this treaty, Afghanistan stepped out of isolation and began establishing diplomatic missions' abroad.[34] The British had been forced to eat the proverbial 'humble pie' and to accept the major demands of the Afghans. Consequently, in the summer of 1920, a delegation from Afghanistan arrived at Missouri, a hill station in India, where they met with the British Indian delegation led by Sir Henry Davis. The discussions dragged on for eleven months and finally on 22 November 1921, a consensus was reached under which, it was agreed, that all previous agreements signed with the Afghan Governments shall be honored by the British. It was also agreed that: [32]

(i) The parties would respect the territorial integrity and independence of each nation.

(ii) Afghanistan and Britain will establish consulates in London and Kabul respectively. In addition, Britain will be allowed to open consulates in Kandahar and Jalalabad, while Afghanistan will have a Consulate General's office located in New Delhi, and smaller consulate offices in Calcutta, Karachi and Bombay.

(iii) In order to facilitate trade and establish postal links, Afghan trade agencies will be established at Peshawar, Quetta and Parachinar in India. To ensure stability in prices, for transit trade between India and Afghanistan, duty and tax rebates shall apply on items stored in bonded warehouses at the border.

(iv) It was also agreed, that if military action is taken against unruly tribes in the north west frontier of India, prior notice shall be provided to the Afghanistan Government.

Following the agreement, Afghanistan established diplomatic relations with the Soviet Union on 28 February 1921.[33] Also, during this period, a delegation comprising representatives of the Ministry of Education, Health and Trade toured a number of European countries. However, the flagrant display of independence was not looked at kindly by the British Government. Consequently, during the delegation's visit to London, when it sought an appointment to meet the Foreign Secretary, it was brusquely asked to contact the India office instead. The Afghans took the insult in stride, and proceeded with establishing diplomatic ties with other countries including Iran and Turkey. In 1922 friendship agreements were signed with the Governments of France, Belgium, Italy and China.

Afghanistan initiated closer contacts with Russia and on 31 August 1926, a friendship pact was signed between the two countries under which it was agreed that:[36]

(i) Both parties would desist from taking any steps which could have an adverse affect on the political climate or the armed forces of either of the two countries.

(ii) The signatories shall not make any agreement with a third country which could conflict with the interest of either of the two countries.

(iii) In the event trade or commercial restrictions are imposed by a third country, then either of the two signatories shall not support these restrictions.

(iv) The signatories shall not interfere in the internal affairs of the other country.

(v) The signatories will ensure that no individual or group activity is allowed directly or indirectly on the soil of their respective countries, which can threaten their independence or sovereignty.

Thus, Amir Amanullah Khan established himself as a strong and able ruler and a powerful head of a central government. He was also aware that in order to change the mindset of his people, education and literacy was a prerequisite. Consequently three new educational institutions on the pattern of Habibia were set up.[35] These were named, Isteqlal, Ghazi and Nijat. The syllabus of these institutions was designed on modern lines which included German and French languages as a part of the curriculum. Unfortunately, his efforts were stymied by shortage of teaching staff and the institutions languished. To offset this disadvantage, a large number of aspiring students, both male and female were sent out to the Universities in foreign countries.

The educational reforms, especially those relating to female emancipation, did not sit well with the religious minded tribes. In 1924 a rebellion broke out against the King but was subdued. Though the security forces succeeded in quelling the rebellion, it sounded the death knell for further reforms.[35] The Amir was deeply disappointed and decided to go on a foreign tour to get away from his troubles.

In 1927 he along with his family, undertook a tour of India, Egypt, Europe, Turkey and Iran. Taking this opportunity, he signed assorted agreements with the governments of the countries he visited. He returned to Afghanistan in middle of 1928, deeply impressed with the cultural and technological progress he witnessed in Europe and particularly in Turkey, under the leadership of Mustafa Kemal Pasha. He decided to continue with his own reforms building on the Turkish model.[36] He made a radio broadcast to the Afghan people, describing the benefits that had accrued to Europe, as a result of the technological and social reforms. He advocated similar reforms in Afghanistan, so that one day the nation could march in step with the developed countries of the world.

To appease the conservative tribes, Amanullah convened a Loya Jirga (gathering of village elders) in which the prominent sardars were invited. He achieved some success but the meeting also fueled controversy.[36] This time the main opposition came from the Shinwari tribe in the east and from a place called Koh Daman in the north led by a highway brigand named Habibullah. His ancestors were known as the 'mashkis' (water carriers) as they used to supply water in goat skins. Habibullah would rob from the rich and give to the poor, Robin Hood style, and was popularly referred to as 'bacha saqa' or 'son of the water carrier.' He led a rag tag mob of religious fundamentalists and attacked the palace. The security guards could not withstand the determined onslaught. Amir Amanullah to save himself, escaped to Kandahar. Bacha Saqa triumphantly declared himself King. His rule was brief and lasted just nine months.[37] During this period anarchy reigned. The royal treasury was looted and untold suffering was inflicted on the populace.

In April 1929, to regain his lost throne, Amanullah attacked Gazni and captured it. But once again his forces could not withstand the counter attack by Bacha Saqa, who not only pushed him out of Gazni but also occupied Kandahar.[38] On 23 May 1929, the broken hearted and defeated Amir Amanullah Khan entered India through Chaman, a border town, stayed in Bombay for a month, and then departed for Italy.

There is no doubt that Amanullah was a patriot and sincerely wanted to implement reforms which would have taken his people out of poverty and backwardness. His lack of success was due to a number of reasons. Firstly, his mission was based on an emotional logic. Impressed by the progress made in Europe and Mustafa Kemal's Turkey, he wanted to replicate it in Afghanistan, forgetting that there was a wide gap in the cultural mores of Turkey and Afghanistan. Turkey, with a high rate of literacy and geographical proximity to Europe, was better equipped to handle the ingredients of progress. Afghanistan on the other hand was a tribal society which was not willing to give up the conservative and deeply religious traditions built up over the centuries.[38] Secondly, Amir Amanullah was no Mustafa Kemal Pasha, the Turkish leader, in ability or determination. The advisors who had the Amir's confidence were mere sycophants out to fill their pockets, with no desire to improve the conditions of the Afghan people.

Amir Nadir Shah

At the time of the defeat of Amir Amanullah Khan, Nadir Khan, the former head of the army, was undergoing treatment in France. He had been appointed to that position by Amir Amanullah's father, Amir Habibullah Khan. Differences developed between Nadir Khan and the Amir over military matters and in 1924, he was removed and posted to France as ambassador. The differences between the two did not abate with the distance. Finally, he resigned as ambassador and took up residence in Nice, France, as a private citizen.

On hearing of Amanullah Khan's defeat, Nadir Khan immediately returned home and started a military campaign against the usurper with the help of former colleagues in the army.[39] On 29 September 1929 Nadir Khan, sent the first contingent of troops under the leadership of his brother Vali Khan and succeeded in capturing Kabul. Bacha Saqa was arrested and put to death. Nadir Khan, declared himself the King, in October 1929, and would henceforth be known as Nadir Shah. He ruled from 1929 through 1933.[40]

Afghanistan's economy, at the time of capture of Kabul by Nadir Khan, was in ruins. Bacha Saqa, in his nine month rule, had destroyed every facet of administration. There was no law and order and the entire country was at the whim and mercy of criminals and brigands. Trade of any kind had been destroyed and the people wandered the streets, in ragged clothes, looking for food.[42] The villages were in even more dire straits than the cities. The treasury was empty and at there was not a single coin in the vaults. The situation was further exacerbated by inter-tribal warfare.

Nadir Shah on assuming power immediately ordered the release of all political prisoners and invited those in exile, to return home. He also realized that his immediate priority was a strong central government and a disciplined military to enforce law and order. He assigned the job to his brother Shah Mahmud who had extensive experience in military matters. In February 1929, the Shinwari and other tribes of Demane Koh (home of Bacha Saqa) as well as the criminal elements of Farghana led by a brigand named Ibrahim Baig rebelled against Nadir Shah. These uprisings were successfully put down by Shah Mahmud, and law and order was once again restored.

After subduing the rebels, Nadir Shah concentrated on bringing reforms to the country. The educational institutions, which had been closed during Bacha Saqa's time, were reopened. In addition, new schools were established and the syllabus revised to meet the requirements of the country. A medical college was set up to meet the future need of doctors. A new hospital was built which was named the Rafiqi Sanatorium.[40] A military academy was also established for training of future officers. Also to introduce the students to Western education, a group of graduates was sent out to America. A Stock Exchange and a bank named the 'National Bank of Afghanistan' were set up. Dams were constructed at six different locations and a road constructed through the Hindu Kush mountain range which connected Kabul to the Mazar and Kitaghan provinces.

A constitution was also drafted defining the roles of the Executive and the Judiciary with a lower and upper house for the country's parliament. These plans, unfortunately, were never implemented in Nadir Shah's lifetime.

An essential endeavour of Nadir Shah was to ensure the independence of Afghanistan while maintaining good relations with both Russia and Britain.[38] On 24 June 1931 a friendship agreement was signed with Russia followed by one with Japan (November 1930) and Ethiopia a month later. In June 1932 friendship treaties were signed with Saudi Arabia and a similar one with Iraq.[40] Nadir Shah's reign ended with his assassination on 8 November 1933.

ZAHIR SHAH, THE LAST AFGHAN KING

Zahir Shah became king on the death of his father. He was born in Kabul on 5 November 1914. His initial education was at the Habibia School while his father, at that time, was the head of the army.[42] In July 1924, he and his mother moved to France, on his father's posting there as ambassador. He enrolled in a number of French schools which included a stint at Lycee Pasteur. Until his return home he was enrolled at the De Montpellier College. After his father occupied the Afghan throne, Zahir Shah returned to Afghanistan in 1930 and enrolled at the Royal Afghan Infantry School. After completion of his training, he was inducted into various governmental duties which included officiating as minister of defense in the absence of his Uncle, Shah Mahmud. He was appointed the minister of defense and a regular member of the cabinet, in 1933, and retained the portfolio until he was crowned King.[43]

At the time of his coronation, Zahir Shah was only 19 years old. He appointed his Uncle Sardar Hashim Khan as the Prime Minister who remained in this position until 1945. At the end of World War II, in which Afghanistan remained neutral, a number of changes took place in the immediate neighbourhood. The Indian sub-continent became independent, after almost 200 years of British rule, and Russia and the United States of America emerged as super powers.

In 1953, the king appointed his brother-in-law, Sardar Daud Khan as his prime minister. Sardar Daud realized that to be successful, his first priority would have to be improvement in the law and order situation. His approach to the problem, unlike his predecessor, was to be tough and ruthless. His efforts were successful and soon peace and tranquility returned to the country.[40] In order to promote reforms, a new ministry of planning and development was set up under the direct stewardship of the premier. A number of five-year-plans were made wherein bulk of the financing came from the Soviet Union and the United States. The first five-year-plan began in 1956 on which 15 billion Afghanis (local currency) were spent. The second five-year-plan began in 1962 which required funding of 44.5 billion Afghanis. Fifty two per cent of the funding was met through external sources.

A notable feature of Zahir Shah's rule was his patronage of educational institutions in the country. As a result, the number of students attending primary schools increased from 273,000 in 1961 to 573,000 in 1972. In 1972 there were 3232 primary schools which was an increase of 6 per cent over the previous year.[43] Correspondingly, the number of middle schools also increased to 497, an increase of 21 per cent. In 1932 the Kabul University came into existence. Initially it started off as a Medical school but by 1975 it had 11 faculties. In 1976 the foundation stone for another teaching University was laid at Jalalabad. In 1975 the students at Kabul University numbered 7000 while the faculty consisted of 974 members. The students and faculty at the Jalalabad University in the same year numbered 410 and 61 respectively.[40]

The King was also keen on promoting female education. In 1959 the Prime Minister, Sardar Daud, with the support of Queen Humaira, started a campaign to bring the women out of Purdah (seclusion) with good results.[43] A large number of women succeeded in obtaining higher education and started taking part in different fields of work. In the 1964, women participated eagerly and some were elected. For the first time in Afghan history, a woman had become a member of the cabinet.

During his premiership, Sardar Daud appointed his brother Sardar Naeem, as the Foreign Minister. Under Sardar Daud's stewardship, the country's foreign policy was vibrant and successful. Afghanistan was presented on the world stage as a non-aligned country. Help came from the United Nations, the US and the Soviet Union.[43] While the Soviets built roads in the North, the Americans built them in the south. A kind of competition ensued between the super powers to win over the country to their sphere of influence. The beneficiary, in this tug of war, was of course Afghanistan. The Kabul government successfully played off one super power against the other. For example, the Soviets were awarded the contract to build the infrastructure of the Kabul airport while the communication and other electronic equipment were supplied by the Americans.

In 1950 America's Import /Export Bank provided loans to the Afghan

Government for development projects in the Helmand Valley. The projects related to agriculture and power generation. Until 30 June 1968, the American aid to Afghanistan amounted to approximately $400 million. Forty five per cent of this amount went towards communication projects, 25 per cent was spent in Helmand Valley and about 12 per cent on education and the remaining 18 per cent on agriculture and administration.[44]

The Soviets too were not far behind in doling out funds. The construction of warehouses for storing grain and the construction of a tunnel through the Hindu Kush Mountains (the Salang tunnel) needs special mention. The tunnel which was opened in 1964 connected North Afghanistan to the Soviet Union.

In the second five-year-plan (1962 to 1967) there was a significant increase in Soviet aid. It constituted 65 per cent of the total foreign aid received by Afghanistan. In comparison, the US component was 23 per cent while West Germany contributed 9 per cent. The balance came from the World Bank.[44] If the third five-year-plan (1967 to 1972) is included in the total, then the foreign aid and loans to Afghanistan between 1950 and 1972 amounted to $1.6 billion out of which the Soviet contribution alone was $1.0 billion. In the period 1972 to 1973 the foreign loans amounted to $608 million of which the Soviet contribution alone was $452 million while the US share was $68 million, and West Germany's contribution was $54 million.[44] The huge spending by the Soviets in Afghanistan was not altruistic. It was a part of a plan to expand their influence and eventually control Afghanistan.

Zahir Shah's rule was an era of peace and prosperity in Afghanistan.[45] He ruled for approximately 40 years (November 1933 to August 1973), during which there were one or two uprisings which were put down quietly and efficiently. Problems began in the 1970s most of which were generated by students and religious leaders. The students were greatly influenced by the teachings of Mao. The movement was not financed or inspired by the Chinese, but was strictly a homegrown variety, promoted by an idealist young generation who had studied Mao's philosophies and thought it to be the panacea for Afghanistan's problems. The student movement was called 'Shola Javed' (the eternal flame) and had a large following in the student community. The manifesto, which was very popular, was based on the following demands:[43]

(i) End of Monarchy and establishment of transparent Democracy.

(ii) End of corruption in the Government.

(iii) Reduction in minimum age for voting in general elections to 18 years.

(iv) End of Soviet interference in Afghanistan's internal affairs.

Besides these demands, the students organized protest meetings at the Kabul University, through the year 1970. The focus was on eradication of nepotism and favouritism in the hiring of the teaching staff. The high rate of joblessness amongst college graduates further exacerbated the situation. The other issue was the intensity of religiosity in the population, driven by a fundamentalist clergy. The anger felt by an ordinary Afghan became evident at the time of the state sponsored 100th birthday celebrations of Lenin. Riots broke out throughout the country. It was sparked by a poem published in the weekly newspaper 'Parcham' (the flag) in which Lenin was placed at par with the Prophet Muhammad.[45] The rioters destroyed property and targeted women wearing immodest Western clothes. Demands were made that wearing of mini-skirts and the education of girls be stopped immediately. The military had to be called out to quell the rioting.

These protests were unacceptable to the Soviet Union who, afterall, had pumped in a lot of money into the country. In the sixth five-year-plan, for example, the Soviets had contributed $550 million. Despite the largesse, they were being reviled as an enemy of the Afghan people, out to destroy the Islamic way of life. The Afghans saw the pattern as similar to the one imposed on the Soviet occupied countries of Central Asia. The Soviets were also critical of the rise of Maoism which they viewed as anti-Soviet. They also saw the rise of Islamic fundamentalism as a threat to the growing Soviet clout in Afghanistan.[46] To consolidate their hold they decided to install a pro-Soviet government which would nip the growing anti-Soviet movements in the bud.

President Sardar Daud Khan

Their plans bore fruit in the shape of Daud Khan. As described in the earlier pages Daud was a brother in law of King Zahir Shah and the prime minister. On 17 July 1973 Sardar Daud with the help of the pro-Soviet military officers took the reins of power in the country, while King Zahir

Shah was in Italy undergoing medical treatment. In the same year, in October, Sardar Daud declared Afghanistan a republic and appointed himself the President. He retained the offices of the prime minister as well as the ministries of defense and foreign affairs and declared Martial Law with a dawn to dusk curfew in Kabul. The airport and the country's borders were closed to travellers. Tanks and armoured cars patrolled the streets in Kabul. Speaking on the radio, Daud declared that until now democracy in the country had been a sham. He promised to bring real democracy to the country and declared Afghanistan an Islamic Republic. Speaking on the subject of foreign policy, he said Afghanistan would continue to be non-aligned and will not sign military pacts with any nation. 'It will adhere strictly with the manifesto of the United Nations and will maintain peace and friendship with all countries of the world'. The only exception he declared 'was Pakistan with which the issue of Pakhtunistan and the boundary between the two nations (Durand line) had yet to be resolved'.[44]

As expected, the Soviet Union was the first country to recognize the new government. The next day, 19 July 1973, India and Czechoslovakia followed suit. Pakistan, despite the antagonistic remarks by Daud, announced its recognition three days later. President Daud abrogated the 1964 constitution and dissolved the parliament. All the powers that the King enjoyed were transferred to the office of the President. A committee was formed to frame a new constitution which was duly completed four months later in November 1976.[45] In December of that year a Loya Jirga, comprising governors of provinces, tribal sardars and a few elite citizens, was requisitioned to review the new constitution. In February 1977, the Jirga approved the constitution by a majority and appointed Sardar Daud as President for a period of six years. The President took the oath the next day. In the new constitution the Quranic Sharia Laws were given supremacy over the civil laws.

BORDER ISSUES WITH PAKISTAN

Until the nineteenth century, there was no border dispute between British India and Russia, as a distance of 1400 miles separated the border, with the nearest Russian occupied territory in Central Asia. The situation began changing in the middle of the nineteenth century, when Russia swiftly occupied wide swaths of land, bordering India and Afghanistan.[65] The expansion southward began in 1839, when under General Count Perovski, Russia attacked Kiva in Uzbekistan. The attack had to be abandoned due to shortage of food supplies and inclement weather. The retreat became a debacle with considerable loss of men and equipment. The Russians began a new offensive and by 1847 had occupied the land right up to the basin of Syr Darya (Darya means Sea/large river in Persian). They also occupied Tashkent the capital city of Uzbekistan in 1865 and two other Uzbek cities, Samarkand and Kiva, in 1868 and 1873 respectively. Russia's last big expansion in Central Asia took place in 1881 when it occupied Turkmenistan.

While Russia expanded in Central Asia, Britain was consolidating its rule in India. Thus Afghanistan was caught in a pincer between Russia and Britain. Being militarily weak, there was not much it could do except watch helplessly from the sidelines. The situation from the Afghan perspective was alarming and they asked the Soviets for demarcation of the boundary. The Soviets agreed and work started on the project in 1885.[46] The boundary commission that was set up included, besides Russia and Afghanistan, a representative of the Government of British India. During the demarcation talks, the ownership of a village named Panjdah became the bone of contention. While the village historically, had belonged to Afghanistan, it had been in the possession of the Russians for the last decade. The Amir of Afghanistan demanded a right of way for his military, which infuriated the Russians. While the negotiations were still in progress, the Russians attacked and killed the Afghans and Indians living in the village. The British viewed the Russian action as provocative and a confrontation became imminent. The Russians began marshalling forces on their side of the border and the British responded by a military buildup in Quetta on the Afghan border.[46] As war became inevitable Amir Abdur Rehman wisely decided to relinquish his claim on Panjdah. He could see that in a conflict, his nation would fare the worst. Tempers cooled, and the commission completed the demarcation in 1887.[47]

After settling the border issue with the Russians, the Amir then proposed a similar delineation of the border with British India. The Viceroy of India Lord Lansdowne agreed and appointed Sir Mortimer Durand as the head of a commission to complete the assignment.[47] The work started in good spirits. Maps were used to determine the divide. An initial agreement was reached and signatures affixed whereby both parties resolved to respect the boundary between their two nations.

After the initial paper work, the demarcation began on site and was completed in two years. The field reports were incorporated in the final agreement, and were duly signed by the two parties. The boundary line agreed to between Afghanistan and British India is known as the Durand Line. It is noteworthy that during the entire rule of Amir Abdur Rahman and his descendents, the agreement's legitimacy was never questioned.[48] The dispute began much later, in the middle of the twentieth century, when India and Pakistan were about to gain independence from Britain.

The Second World War had taken its toll and Britain, reeling from the economic costs of the War, no longer had the will or the resources to rule India. Also, America and Russia, the two new superpowers, were in favour of freedom for the Indian sub-continent.[49]

Before the two new nations India and Pakistan came into existence, Afghanistan decided to stake its claim to a large territory in British India, adjacent to its border. The argument was that the area historically, was a part of Afghanistan, and that the Durand Line which was agreed to in 1893, was no longer valid as the British were now leaving.

The Afghan claim was received by the Indian Government in 1946, at a time when as a result of the recent elections an interim Government had been formed, of which Jawaharlal Nehru was the Foreign Minister. He rejected the claim out of hand and declared the Durand Line as the legal boundary between India and Afghanistan. Mr. Nehru also warned Afghanistan that if they persisted, then India too shall lodge a counter claim, as a large territory of Afghanistan had historically been a part of India.[51]

Pakistan came into existence on 14 August 1947 and as a successor to Britain, it inherited the obligations and rights to all agreements signed by the government of British India. After the formation of Pakistan, the Afghan Government claimed a wide swath of Pakistan territory, located in its North Western Province. They also claimed a special relationship with the Pashtu speaking Pathan population across the border, who Kabul said, were being held hostage by Pakistan. The Pakistan Government, in return, reminded them that in the 1947 referendum, held by the British India Government, the population of the North West Frontier Province had voted overwhelmingly (99%) for joining Pakistan.[52]

King Zahir Shah, in contrast to Prime Minister Daud Khan, was a peace loving man and had no animus with Pakistan. He was in favour of peaceful relations between the two countries. Sardar Daud's stance however, was totally different. During the ten years of his stewardship as prime minister (1953 to 1963), his sole preoccupation was to somehow revive the 'pakhtunistan' controversy, as it served to divert the attention of the people from more urgent internal issues. The situation gradually mellowed down and a change in the relations came about in 1976, when President Daud became preoccupied with the worsening relations with the Soviet Union.

LOYA JIRGA

The concept of Loya Jirga in Afghanistan, and for the Pashtuns living across the border in Pakistan, goes back a long time in history. It is traditionally a gathering of tribal chiefs and elders of the society. It has a law dispensing authority and enjoys the same respect and authority as a Supreme Court in the Anglo-Saxon cultures. In the October 1964 constitution, the Parliament consisted of an upper and a lower house and the Loya Jirga included members from both houses, as well as the Governors of provinces. The Loya Jirga is a permanent institution, and its role is not affected, even if the Parliament is dissolved. It can however be convened, only under a 'firman' (order) of the King or the President. The members of the Loya Jirga enjoy the same privileges as the members of the parliament. They are immune from prosecution by any civil court in the country and can be tried and punished only by the Jirga, and that too by two-third majority vote.[52]

Until the abdication of Zahir Shah, the Loya Jirga acted under the rules of the 1964 Constitution. However, the rules changed when Sardar Daud became President. The members of the dismissed Parliament were no longer considered members of the Jirga. However, since approval by the Jirga of all major decisions by the government was mandatory, which included Sardar Daud's own appointment as president, he modified the Jirga by limiting the membership to a few pliable governors of provinces and supportive elite.

DAUD'S GOVERNANCE

It is true that unlike Zahir Shah, Sardar Daud was no longer neutral in his policies, and in fact leaned towards the Soviet Union. After all, he owed his present position to the support from the Soviets and their protégés in the Afghan military. His leftist leanings, however, became the bête noire of the rightist religious elements. He ultimately proved a disappointment to the Soviets also, as they had expected him to form a socialist setup similar to the one prevalent in the Soviet satellite countries of Central Asia. Sardar Daud instead preached democracy, but at the same time opposed the formation of multiple political parties. Nepotism in the military also became a factor in the buildup of resentment against him. Sardar Daud belonged to the Muhammad Zai tribe whose members were given preferential treatment in hiring and promotions. The policy alienated officers who belonged to other tribes.[54]

The Communist party of Afghanistan called 'The Parcham' party, was under Soviet tutelage and under a well thought out plan, had bought the loyalties of many officers in the military. Daud was aware of the brewing conspiracies and to thwart them had purged the army of a large number of suspect officers which included the head of the air force who was replaced in 1973. The changes made were too little and too late as by then the communists had tightened their hold into a throttle.[55]

Fearing reprisals, Sardar Daud from 1975 onwards, started withdrawing from the Soviets. He had at last concluded that the Soviet largesse was not without strings and that a military intervention against his government was imminent. The Soviets retaliated by stopping all aid to the country, causing an economic crisis. Sardar Daud turned to the Shah of Iran for assistance and during the visit of the Secretary General of the Islamic conference to Kabul also asked for similar assistance from Muslim nations including Saudi Arabia and Kuwait. He also softened his aggressive stance against Pakistan and the border issues were put on the back burner. Stalled relations with the US and China were revived and In 1975, Dr. Henry Kissinger, the US Secretary of State visited Kabul which was followed by a visit to China by Daud's brother and Foreign Minister Sardar Naeem.

Besides political issues, dispute in trade matters was also a factor in the worsening relations with the Soviets. Afghanistan tripled its price of natural gas supplied to the Soviet Republics in Central Asia, and also cancelled the franchise given to the Soviets for its dry fruit. These and other acts spurred the Soviets to act quickly to remove Daud from power. They chose Nur Muhammad Taraki as his potential replacement.[56]

On 27 April 1978 Sardar Daud was removed by an army coup d'état. The army contingent that took over the presidential palace was led by a 37-year-old Lieutenant Colonel named Abdul Qadir. Radio Kabul started referring to him as General-Qadir immediately after the coup. Both Sardar Daud and his brother Sardar Naeem, the foreign minister, were killed in the fighting that ensued.

According to William Crowley, the BBC correspondent in Kabul,[57] Sardar Daud had been informed of a possible coup on the morning of 27 April 1978. Within the hour he had 50 tanks and anti-aircraft guns positioned around the palace. He then called an emergency cabinet meeting at 10a.m. that morning, which included the cabinet ministers, military commanders as well as the Commander in Chief of the country's Air Force. The discussions focused on measures to defeat the insurgency. It is believed that the rebels had originally planned the attack on the night between 27 April and 28 April. On hearing of the cabinet meeting, the rebels decided to bring the coup forward to 27 April at 11.30 a.m. The Presidential palace was encircled by rebel tanks as the rebel air attacks began. A former pilot of the Afghan Air Force, who at that time was staying at a nearby hotel, told Crawley, that the bombing was so precise that the pilots could only have been Russians. The fighting lasted until the morning of 28 April, when Kabul radio announced the death of President Daud and the formation of a new Government led by the Revolutionary Council which was immediately recognized by the Soviet Union, North Vietnam, Yugoslavia, North Yemen and East Germany. Pakistan, the next door neighbour, announced its recognition a week later.[57]

President Noor Muhammad Taraki

Nur Muhammad Taraki, the Soviet anointed leader of the revolution, appeared on the scene a few days later, when the Revolutionary Council named him the Chairman, Prime Minister and the President of the Republic.[58] In September 1979, Taraki had attended a conference of non-aligned nations in Havana. On the way back, he stopped in Moscow and met the Soviet General Secretary, Lenoid Breznev when it was agreed that:[59]

- In view of the increased activity of the freedom fighters (Mujahideen), the Taraki Government should also initiate a political dialogue with the rebels besides military confrontation.
- Bring back Babrak Karmal, the Afghan Ambassador in

Czechoslovakia, to Kabul and appoint him the Prime Minister in place of Hafizullah Amin, the current Prime Minister.

On his return to Kabul, Taraki received reports that the Prime Minister Hafizullah Amin, had been tipped off and was planning his own coup. Taraki immediately ordered his arrest and assigned an army team to carry it out. On 14 September 1979, before the arrest could be made, the Peoples House where Taraki had his offices was bombed. Cannons were fired on the building killing a large number of the staff. President Taraki was seriously injured. In the early morning of 9 October 1979 Taraki was killed purportedly on the orders of the politburo. According to an official at the Ministry of Defense, Taraki had been strangled to death on the orders of Hafizullah Amin.[58]

PRESIDENT HAFIZULLAH AMIN

On 16 September 1979, following the death of Taraki, the Central Committee of the Peoples Democratic Party of Afghanistan announced that Hafizullah Amin had been unanimously appointed the Prime Minister, Minister of Defense and Secretary General of the Party. A few hours later it was announced that he had also been appointed the head of the revolutionary council. The same day another announcement was made that actually President Taraki, due to mental and other medical problems, had wished to resign from the party high command and that at his request, Hafizullah Amin had been appointed in his place.

In Moscow, the Soviet News Agency, *The Tass*, reported the news of Taraki's resignation on 16 September 1979. 'Pravda' the official Soviet newspaper published the news item the next day.[60] The Soviets apparently supported the new Government and promised continuation of aid. Both President Breznev and Prime Minister Alexi Kosygin sent messages of felicitations to Hafizullah Amin who had designated himself both as president and prime minister. He also retained the portfolios of the ministry of defense and intelligence and inducted his brother Abdullah Amin in the cabinet.[60]

With the installation of Amin as President, there began an era of uncertainty in Afghanistan as a result of which there was a large exodus of refugees to Pakistan. It is estimated that approximately 200,000 Afghan citizens moved to Pakistan immediately after Amin's assumption of power. His regime was shaky from the start, as attested by the fact that within 3 months of his takeover, numerous conspiracies were hatched to dislodge him from power.

While everything looked in order on the surface, the Soviet Union was a deeply unhappy with the turn of events in Afghanistan. They had wanted Babrak Karmal as the Prime Minister and were preparing grounds for the transfer of power from Taraki to Karmal when Amin stepped in and upset their plans. Consequently, while the Soviets put up a show of goodwill for the new government, they were not willing to accept Amin as the new leader. They could not forgive Amin, for the cold-blooded murder of Taraki, who after all, was once their protégé.

Amin therefore had good reasons to expect retribution from the Soviets sooner or later. Consequently, immediately after toppling Taraki, he demanded that Moscow replace its current ambassador in Kabul on the grounds that his stay in the country had been too long. He put in place his own security force as he no longer trusted the pro-Soviet army officers.

After the coup Moscow had pressured Amin to invite Soviet troops to Afghanistan to crush the Islamic fundamentalists. Amin refused to oblige the Soviets.[60] To further strengthen his position, Amin established secret contacts with the Americans and other Western nations. His son-in-law, who was the head of Afghan intelligence, was instrumental in making these contacts. Amin was naïve in believing that he could take on the Soviets and get away with it. After all, the Soviet Union was not about to let go of the country in which they had invested over $ 1.5 billion over the last 20 years. The Soviets had also infiltrated the military with over one thousand Soviet advisors, now based in Kabul, in preparation for takeover of the country.

On 19 September 1979 fighting broke out at the Presidential Palace in which Amin was shot and injured by a pro-Soviet Afghan army officer. Amin was arrested by the army and imprisoned at the former Royal Palace, 'Darul Aman'. After a brief show trial, he was condemned to death and hanged on 27 September 1979. Shortly thereafter Babrak Karmal was declared the new President by the Revolutionary Council.[61]

President Babrak Karmal

Karmal was born on 6 January 1929. After graduation from high school in 1948, he joined the Kabul University to study law. He was still a student when he became a member of the Afghan Communist Party. He was arrested in 1950 for political activities and imprisoned for five years. After release from the prison, he went back to the University and joined the military for one year. In 1957 he was hired by the Government in the Ministry of Planning, where he was employed for eight years. While working for the Government he became involved in politics and joined the pro-Soviet Parcham party. He was elected to the parliament twice, in 1965 and 1969 respectively. He remained in the parliament until the abolishment of monarchy in 1973. It is noteworthy that Babarak Karmal and Taraki had always worked closely as comrades, promoting communism in the country. In fact when Taraki became President, he appointed Babarak Karmal as the Vice chairman of the revolutionary council as well as Prime minister of the country. This did not sit well with Hafizullah Amin who succeeded in persuading Taraki, that all cabinet members associated with Parcham party were disloyal to the president as they were too close to the Soviets, and therefore a threat. Taraki, at Amin's behest, then sent Karmal away as ambassador to Czechoslovakia and appointed Amin as prime minister in his place.

Babrak Karmal as President can best be described as a Soviet puppet. He was President for almost seven years beginning in 1979 until 1986, when the Soviets replaced him with Dr. Najibullah and thereafter, left for Moscow, where he eventually died. His body was brought back to Afghanistan for burial.

Babrak Karmal will be remembered in history as the 'Quisling' of Afghanistan, who in December 1979 invited the Soviet Union to occupy his own country.

President Dr. Najibullah

Najibullah (like many Afghans, he only had one name) was a great survivor at a time of particular turbulence in Afghanistan. Installed as president in 1986 during the Soviet occupation of his country, he clung to power until 1992— for nearly three years after the Soviet Red Army had pulled back all its troops.[91] He met a violent end at the hands of the Taliban just hours after their forces had swept up from the east and captured Kabul. Najibullah and his brother were pulled out of a United Nations compound, shot and their bodies strung up on a pole outside the presidential palace. The manner of their deaths outraged Norbert Hall, the head of the United

Nations mission to Afghanistan, who promptly issued a statement expressing dismay that the brothers were killed without a legitimate trial. Holl said that the murder violated international law, and jeopardized efforts to secure a peaceful settlement in Afghanistan.[90]

Najibullah (whose name means "noble man of god") was born in 1947 to a middle-class Pashtun family in Gardez, in the eastern provincial province of Paktia, and spent much of his childhood in the Pakistani frontier town of Peshawar. His father was a government official representing the Afghan government in Peshawar with a brief to cultivate contacts among the warring tribes of the frontier, giving the young Najibullah his first lessons in politics.

He graduated from high school in Kabul in 1965, and then spent 10 years studying medicine. He qualified, but never practiced medicine. At the university he became a student leader of the Parcham wing of the fledgling Communist Party and was jailed once for leading an egg-throwing attack on the car of Spiro Agnew, the former United States vice-president, who was visiting Afghanistan. A big man, Najibullah earned his nickname, the Ox, while at university, where he developed a keen interest in weightlifting and wrestling.

During the years of supremacy of the other wing of the Afghan Communist Party, the Khalq wing, Najibullah was sent into virtual exile, along with other Parcham leaders. He became ambassador to Iran, but absconded to Eastern Europe, only to resurface again in Afghanistan in 1979, when he returned to Kabul with Babrak Karmal, the new president, leading a government, supported by Moscow and dominated by the communist Parcham faction.[88]

His loyalty to the Soviets was rewarded when he was made head of the KGB-trained secret police, known as Khad in 1979. It was a position he was to hold until he took over as president in 1986 (formally from the following year) from Karmal, who stepped down and left the country, ostensibly on health grounds. When the last Soviet troops pulled out of Afghanistan in February 1989, there was an almost unanimous prediction that Najibullah would soon fall. Diplomats predicted that the Mujahideen, who had fought against the now- departed Red Army, would topple Najibullah within a matter of months. But he managed to cling on not least, because of the almost total inability of the diverse Mujahideen factions to fight together against their infidel foe.[90]

Najibullah, who had espoused Communism during the Soviet period, also changed his ideological spots to suit the times. He was, however, widely hated, not least because of his links with the Soviet leadership, but more for his reputation as head of the secret police, where he allegedly tortured and killed hundreds of his enemies. A highly intelligent man, he was reputed to understand his countrymen better than almost any other Afghan leader, before or since. Many governments eventually came to feel that Najibullah had a firm pair of hands that might well have held Afghanistan together.

But his fall from power and subsequent incarceration in the UN compound in Kabul were a result of a fairly extraordinary succession of events. Najibullah agreed in UN-sponsored talks that he would step down to make way for an interim administration, which included the very people he had been fighting against. On the day the talks were scheduled, as he was on the way to the venue, one of his main commanders, General Abdur Rashid Dostam, swapped sides to join the Mujahideen forces. As a result of this defection, Najibullah's position in Kabul became untenable, and the UN special representative, Benon Sevan, tried to get him out of the capital. A convoy of UN cars was sent to pick up Najibullah after midnight to take him to the airport on 16 April 1992. But he was turned back from the airport by troops loyal to Dostum, and forced to take refuge in a UN compound until his capture by the Taliban.

The UN had for all the intervening period tried to get him safe passage out of Afghanistan to join his wife and three daughters abroad, but without success. Kabul was largely destroyed in the civil war between the warring factions, after Najibullah's fall from power. People in the city, who strongly disliked him while he was president, would often say that they wished he was still in charge.[91]

3

Soviet Invasion of Afghanistan

Soviet invasion of Afghanistan took place at a time when the Islamic world was in ferment and was in the process of radicalization. It was perceived by the expanding pan-Islamic forces as a political and religious challenge. The Soviet intrusion was seen as occupation by non-Muslim forces of a Muslim country. The apprehension of most Muslim countries was that the Soviet Union will encourage and support left-of-centre political forces in the Islamic world. US and Western democracies along with the Sheikhdoms and Kingdoms of the Gulf considered the Soviet foothold in Afghanistan as a major strategic threat to the sea lanes and trade routes between Asia on the one hand and Europe and North America on the other.[65] The safety of the Western politico-military presence in the Gulf was considered threatened by the Soviet foothold in Afghanistan. There was also a serious apprehension about the security and exploitability of oil and other energy sources in the Gulf over which the Western democracies had consolidated total control since the end of the First World War.

The failure of the Americans to prevent the Iranian revolution and President Carter's failure to rescue the American embassy staff in Tehran made it necessary that the US restore its credibility amongst its Muslim allies in South Asia and the Gulf countries. By the middle of 1980 joint plans were drawn up and operation initiated against the Soviet forces and the Government in Afghanistan. About two and a half to three million refugees had fled into Pakistan with the arrival of the Soviet forces.[65] This became a fertile ground for recruiting personnel for the Afghan resistance. Saudi Arabia, Libya, Egypt and Pakistan joined hands to subvert the communist regime and to pressurize the Soviet regime to withdraw its troops. Pakistan's ISI, the American CIA and the Saudi Intelligence decided on institutional cooperation to organize and sustain the anti-Soviet forces in Afghanistan. The resistance was not only from amongst the Afghans but by 1981 about 2000 to 3000 Saudis, Egyptians, Libyans, Sudanese and volunteer Mujahideen from other Muslim countries had joined the resistance. The number of these foreign mercenaries which also included Osama bin Laden and his al-Qaeda members eventually reached 30,000.[66]

The period between December 1979 and 1984, when Brezhnev passed away, saw the Soviet forces consolidating their position in Afghanistan and showing a capacity to neutralize the Mujahideen efforts against them. The Soviet Union seemed determined to maintain a long term presence in Afghanistan. Iran on one hand, China on the other, was equally opposed to the Soviet intrusion into Afghanistan. Iran apprehended subversion against the Iranian revolution from Soviet dominated Afghanistan. China was only concerned about the Soviet presence at the extremity of Southern Asia posing a politico-military threat to western Tibet and Sinkiang.

The situation in Afghanistan towards the end of 1981 was that the Soviet troops dominated the country and the Afghan Government was in control of the major cities and townships. The countryside however, witnessed continuing conflict and skirmishes between the Soviet and Afghan troops on one hand and various Mujahideen groups on the other. The Mujahideen were being supplied with money, arms and equipment as well as logistical support from the Pakistan territory.[66] The Afghan resistance groups were not a unified entity. The main group was led by Rabbani, Mujaddadi, Saiaf and Gulbadin Hekmatyar. All these groups had their bases in townships in Pakistan on the Afghan border. The other group resisting the Soviets, and located within Afghanistan, was led by a Tajik guerilla leader, Ahmed Shah Masud who had entrenched himself in the Panjsher Valley.[66]

TALIBAN—THE HOLY WARRIORS

After almost ten years of occupation, the Soviet Union, reeling under significant losses in men as well as its economic plight at home, decided to withdraw its troops from Afghanistan, in February 1989. The

Government of the Peoples Democratic Party of Afghanistan was disbanded and the President, Babrak Karmal, and the majority of the Politburo went into exile. The Taliban started operating as a military force some time towards the end of 1995. The ranks of the Taliban movement consisted of recruits from Pashtun youth from Pakistan and from South Western Afghanistan. The word Pashtun derives from the word Pashtu, a language spoken by approximately fifty percent of the population of Afghanistan.[67] The remaining population consists of the Tajiks, Hazaras and the Uzbeks. The leftist revolution failed in Afghanistan after tenuous attempts to sustain it with Russian support for a period of ten years from 1979 to 1989. It failed because it did not capture the imagination of the Afghan people nor did it succeed in transcending the ethnic factions of the Afghan civil society. The shared vision of resisting the Soviet intrusion into Afghanistan and establishing a truly nationalistic government fragmented the moment Russian withdrawal was fulfilled. The consequence was the rise of the Taliban. The Taliban itself had several factions consisting of recruits from Baluchistan, the North West Frontier of Pakistan, madrasas or religious institutions, former Mujahideens, who defected to the Taliban as well as the former members of the Afghan militia.[67] By 1995, other Political groups emerged on the Afghan political scene—the Northern Alliance consisting of members of the Uzbek and Tajik militia and Hizb-e-Wahadat representing the interests of the Hazara Shia community supported by Iran. The post Soviet Afghan political scene saw the rise of ethno-centric rival nationalistic impulses centred on Pashtun versus non-Pashtun antagonisms. The interesting ingredients of the Taliban beliefs were, first, that politics divides society and therefore democracy is irrelevant to Afghan society. Secondly, the primary task of governance is to ensure security for the people. Thirdly, social and political order should be rooted in Islam. The majority of the Taliban cadres were Pashtuns. Apart from them, recruits came in from Islamic organizations from number of Muslim countries stretching from Libya and Egypt in the North to Sudan and the Gulf in the South. The Taliban were equipped by the US with sophisticated artillery and anti-aircraft weapons apart from the armour. They believed that the state structures and political management of civil societies should be organized on the basis of orthodox tenets of Islam, the Hadith and the Sharia.[68] They believed that both civil and criminal laws should be rooted in Sunni Islamic theology. In the initial years the Taliban showed great capacity for discipline, austerity, military decisiveness and at times a high level of violence. By the end of 1998, the Taliban had established control over 29 provinces of Afghanistan leaving just the Panjsher valley and Mazar-e-Sharif under the control of the rival Mujahideen leaders. Taliban imposed a strict and orthodox Islamic regime in all areas under their control. The Sharia became the supreme law in Afghanistan. Orthodox Islamic personal and social behaviour became mandatory. Males were required to grow beards and women were to be under strict purdah (seclusion). Women's education and employment was banned. Criminal justice was banned on the stipulations of the Sharia law and implemented by the clergy and the Taliban with ferocious promptness. It must, however, be said to the credit of the Taliban that there was a sharp decline in crime and corruption. The law and order situation improved though on the basis of draconian measures.[68]

Enter Osama bin Laden

In 1986, three years prior to the Soviet with drawl from Afghanistan, the then CIA chief William Casey had persuaded the US Congress to provide the Mujahideen with American 'stinger' missiles to shoot down the Soviet planes and provide US advisors to train the guerillas. Casey committed CIA support to a long standing Pakistani Intelligence (ISI) initiative to recruit radical Muslims from around the world to come to Pakistan and fight alongside the Afghan Mujahideen. Washington wanted to demonstrate that the entire Muslim world was fighting the Soviet Union alongside the Afghan and their American benefactors. None of the players in this game, reckoned on the volunteers having their own agenda, which would eventually, turn their hatred against the Soviets on to the Americans. Between 1982 and 1992 some thirty five thousand radicals from 43 Islamic countries in the Middle East, North and East Africa, Central Asia and the Far East would pass their baptism under fire with the Afghan Mujahideen. Tens of thousands more Muslim radicals came to study in the hundreds of new madrasas set up in Pakistan along the Afghan border. Eventually more than 100,000 Muslim radicals were to have direct contact with Pakistan and Afghanistan and be influenced by the jihad.[69] Amongst these thousands of foreign recruits was a young Saudi student Osama bin Laden, the son of a Yemeni construction magnate Mohammed Bin Laden who was a close friend of the late King Feisal and whose company had become fabulously wealthy on the contracts to renovate the Holy Mosques of Mecca and Medina. Osama bin Laden was born around 1957 the seventeenth of 57 children by his Yemeni father and a Saudi mother, one of Mohammed bin Laden's many wives. He was thin and 6 feet 5 inches tall with long limbs and a flowing beard. After Iraqi invasion of Kuwait, he lobbied with the Saudi royal family to organize a popular defense of the Kingdom and raise a force from the Afghan war veterans to fight Iraq. The Saudis instead invited in the Americans. Bin Laden openly criticized the Royal family and started lobbying the religious *ulemas*, religious scholars, to issue rulings against non-Muslims based in the country. Bin Laden was declared persona non-grata by the Saudi Royal family and he left for Sudan to take part in the Islamic revolution underway under the Sudanese leader Hasan Turabi. Bin Laden's continued criticism of the Saudi royal family eventually annoyed them so much that they revoked his citizenship. While based in Sudan he often travelled to Afghanistan, where he set up an entity called the 'Bureau of Services' or Maktab al Khidmat.[69] This bureau operated a recruiting network in Muslim countries throughout the Middle East, Southeast Asia, Western Europe and the United States. It provided travel funds and guest houses in Pakistan for recruits and volunteers on the road to the Afghan battlefield. Bin Laden also used his financial network to set up training camps and procure weapons and supplies for Arab fighters. Major Afghan warlords who led forces in the battle against the Soviets also benefited from the use of these camps. Following the defeat of the Soviets in the late 1980s, bin Laden formed an organization called 'The Foundation' or al-Qaeda—which was to serve as a foundation upon which to build a global Islamic army. In 1989, the regime in Sudan, run by a military faction and an Islamic extremist organization called the National Islamic Front, invited bin Laden to move there. He sent an advance team to Sudan in 1990 and moved there in mid-1991. Bin Laden brought resources to Sudan, building roads and helping to finance the government's war against separatists in the south.[69] In return, he received permission to establish commercial enterprise and an operational structure to support activities of al-Qaeda. In Sudan, bin Laden built upon the al-Qaeda organization he had established back in Afghanistan. Al-Qaeda had its own membership roster and a structure of 'committees' to guide and oversee such functions as military training, financing operations and issuing edicts to justify al-Qaeda actions. Included in the structure were:[69]

- A Political Committee issuing edicts purporting to be grounded in Islamic Law.
- A Military Committee responsible for gathering ideas and managing training camps.

- A Finance Committee responsible for fund raising and budgetary support for training camps, housing costs, living expenses, travel and money allocated to operations.
- A Foreign Purchases Committee responsible for acquiring weapons and technical equipment.
- A Security Committee responsible physical protection, intelligence gathering and counter intelligence; and an Information Committee in charge of propaganda.

With al-Qaeda as its foundation, bin Laden sought to build a broader Islamic army that also included groups from Egypt, Libya, Algeria, Saudi Arabia and Morocco, Oman, Tunisia, Jordan, Iraq, Lebanon, Somalia and Eritrea. Not all groups from these states agreed to join, but at least one from each did. With a multinational council intended to promote common goals, this Islamic force represented a new level of collaboration among diverse groups. Bin Laden set up training camps, weapons and supply depots in Sudan. He used them to support al-Qaeda and other members of the Islamic army. Bin Laden's operatives also used their positions in his businesses to acquire weapons and technical equipment such as surveillance devices. At this time al-Qaeda's operational role was mainly to provide funds and military training.

Contrary to popular understanding, Bin Laden did not fund al-Qaeda through a personal fortune and a network of businesses. Instead al-Qaeda relied primarily on a fundraising network developed over time. Bin Laden never received a $300 million inheritance. From about 1970 until approximately 1994, he received about $1 million per year—a significant sum, but hardly a $300million fortune that could be used to fund a global jihad. According to Saudi officials and representatives of the Bin Laden family, Osama bin Laden was divested of his share of his family's wealth. Osama bin Laden owned a number of businesses and other assets in Sudan, although most were small and not economically viable.[69]

LAUNCHING ATTACKS ON AMERICAN ASSETS

A December 1992 explosion outside two hotels in Aden, Yemen—a stopover for US troops en route to Somalia killed one Australian tourist but no Americans. US intelligence would learn four years later that the attack was carried out by a Yemeni terrorist group whose leader was close to bin Laden, and whose members reportedly trained at a bin Laden—

funded camp in Sudan that was run by a member of the al-Qaeda Military Committee.

In October 1993, two Black Hawk helicopters were shot down and 18 US soldiers were killed in Mogadishu, Somalia. US intelligence learned in the ensuing years that bin Laden's organization had been heavily engaged in assisting warlords who attacked US forces in Somalia.[70] The head of the al-Qaeda Military Committee, from a command centre set up in Nairobi, Kenya, reportedly sent scores of trainers into Somalia including experts in the use of rocket propelled grenades, the same kind of weapons used to shoot down the helicopters. Operatives dispatched to Somalia were told their mission was to kill US troops, incite violence against US personnel, and undermine the success of the US mission. Sources have described several of these operatives bragging that their work had caused the defeat of the Americans. Bin Laden and his associates attributed the subsequent withdrawal of US forces from Somalia in March 1994 as a victory for the Mujahideen and a demonstration that the Americans could be forced to retreat.

Two additional attacks on US forces in Saudi Arabia took place in 1995-96 for which the evidence of bin Laden's involvement is ambiguous. On 13 November 1995, a car bomb exploded in Riyadh outside the office of Program Management of the US trained Saudi Arabian National Guard. Five Americans and two officials from India were killed. Saudi authorities arrested four suspects, whom they quickly convicted and beheaded.[70] The Saudis televised confessions of three perpetrators including that their actions had been influenced by bin Laden, but there was no charge that bin Laden was directly involved. Later in a March 1997 CNN interview, bin Laden denied responsibility for the attack but said he was sorry he had not been a participant. By this time US intelligence learned that a year and a half before the bombing of Saudi National Guard, al-Qaeda leaders and members of other aligned groups had decided to attack US targets in Saudi Arabia and directed a team to ship explosives there. Bin Laden and his organizations role in this attack however, remain unproven. On 26 June 1996, an explosion ripped through a building in Khobar towers apartment complex housing US Air Force personnel in Dahran, Saudi Arabia. Nineteen Americans were killed and 372 others were injured. Subsequent investigation concluded that the attack had been carried out by a Saudi Shia Hizbullah group with assistance from Iran.[70] Intelligence obtained shortly after the bombing, however, also supported suspicions of bin Laden's involvement. Bin Laden also explored possible cooperation with Iraq during his time in Sudan, despite his opposition to Saddam's secular regime. Bin laden had in fact at one time sponsored anti-Saddam Islamists in Iraqi Kurdistan. The Sudanese, to protect their own ties with Iraq persuaded bin Laden to cease this support and arranged for contacts between Iraq and al-Qaeda. Bin Laden is said to have requested space to establish training camp, as well as assistance in procuring weapon, but Iraq never responded.[70] There is no evidence that ties ever existed between al-Qaeda and Iraq or that they cooperated on attacks against the United States.

In May 1996, bin Laden left Sudan and moved back to Afghanistan where he struck friendship with Mullah Omar the Afghan leader, and thus came under the protection of Taliban. His departure from Sudan resulted from a combination of pressures from the United States, other Western governments, and Egypt, Saudi Arabia and Libya, all three of which faced indigenous terrorist groups supported by bin Laden. The pressure on Sudan intensified in April 1996 when the UN sanctioned Sudan for harboring individuals from the group that had attempted to assassinate Egyptian President Mubarak in June 1995. It was not until later in 1996, however, after he was back in Afghanistan, that new sources disclosed the nature of his organizational structure and its involvement in attacks that had already been carried out on US assets.

Bin Laden's departure from Sudan marked a setback for him. The Saudi government had frozen his assets three years earlier, and the Sudanese government expropriated his assets there after he left Sudan. The financial stresses contributed to strained relations with some of his associates, who used the move back to Afghanistan as an occasion to break from al-Qaeda.[70] There were nevertheless some benefits to the move. In an effort to reduce external pressures, Sudan had made some efforts to keep bin Laden under control and prohibited him from making public diatribes. Afghanistan's lack of a central government gave him greater latitude to promote his own agenda. Moreover, al-Qaeda had never entirely left the region: even when headquartered in Sudan, it had used Afghanistan as a regional base and training centre supporting jihadi movements in Tajikistan, Kashmir and Chechnya.

In August 1996 bin Laden made public his war against the United States. In his 'Declaration of Holy War on the Americans Occupying the

Country of the Two Sacred Places' (Mecca and Medina in Saudi Arabia), bin Laden called on the Muslims worldwide to put aside their differences and join in the attacks to compel the US to withdraw from the Arabian peninsula.

A month after this declaration, the Taliban seized control of Kabul, the nation's capital, and bin Laden began cementing his ties with Taliban; they soon had a close alliance. The Taliban paid a great price for this alliance in the form of outside pressure, isolation U.N. sanctions, and, after 9/11, the destruction of the regime. But prior to 9/11, the Taliban also benefited from its relationship with al-Qaeda: bin Laden provided significant financial support to the Taliban, and supplied hundreds, if not thousands, of fighters to support the Taliban in its ongoing war against other factions in northern Afghanistan. From al-Qaeda's perspective, the alliance provided a sanctuary in which to train and indoctrinate the recruits, import weapons, forge ties with other jihadi groups and leaders and plan terrorist operations. Al-Qaeda fighters could travel freely within the country; enter and exit without visas or any immigration procedures; and enjoy the use of official Afghan Ministry of Defense license plates. Al-Qaeda also used the Afghan state owned Ariana Airlines to courier money into the country. There were also ideological ties. Both the Taliban and bin Laden espoused the vision of a pure Islamic state. Bin Laden reportedly swore an oath of loyalty to the Taliban leader Mullah Omar. Relations between bin Laden and the Taliban leadership were sometimes tense, and some Taliban leaders opposed the al-Qaeda presence. In the end, however, Mullah Omar never broke with bin Laden and Al-Qaeda. By early 1998, Bin Laden was also in the early stages of what would become a merger of his al-Qaeda and another major terrorist group, the Egyptian Islamic Jihad.[69] On 23 February 1998, Bin Laden and the leader of the Egyptian Islamic Jihad, Ayman Zawahiri, published a 'fatwa' that announced a 'ruling to kill the Americans and their allies'. It was also signed by the heads of the three other groups, but their signatures were more a matter of show than substance. Unlike earlier statements, this 'fatwa' explicitly instructed followers to kill 'civilians and military'.

On 7 August 1998 nearly simultaneous truck bombs ravaged the US embassies in the East African capitals of Nairobi, Kenya, and Dares-Salaam, Tanzania. The Nairobi embassy was destroyed, and 213 people were killed, including 12 Americans. About 5,000 people were injured. In Dares-Salaam, 11 more were killed, none of them American, and 85 were injured.[69] US intelligence learned a few months later that the targeting of the US embassy in Nairobi began in late 1993. It was one of more than a dozen potential targets analyzed by a team with the same Nairobi cell used to provide assistance to Somalis. In January 1994, al-Qaeda leaders concluded that the US embassy would be an easy strike. Preparations for the attack did not begin in earnest until late spring 1998, and the bombs were assembled only a few days before the attack. By the night before the embassy bombing, all al-Qaeda members except the suicide squads and a few people assigned to clean up the evidence trail had left East Africa. Bin Laden and other al-Qaeda leaders in Afghanistan had also left for the countryside in expectation of US retaliation. The attacks on the US embassies in East Africa in the summer of 1998 demonstrated a new operational form—they were planned, directed and executed by al-Qaeda—under the direct supervision of bin Laden and his chief aides.[69] After the August 1998 bombing in East Africa, US pressure on the Saudi's increased to persuade the Taliban to hand over bin Laden. Mullah Omar refused to do so. In retaliation the Saudis stopped all further aid to the Taliban. On 12 October 2000, an explosives-laden boat tore through the side of USS Cole anchored in Aden, Yemen. Seventeen members of the Cole crew were killed, and another 39 were wounded. In the course of the ensuing investigation, US officials learnt that an earlier attempt to attack a US warship had been made in January 2000, aimed at the USS Sullivan, but had failed because the attack boat was overloaded with explosives and sank.[69] The boat was salvaged, a new martyr crew was selected, and the attack was successfully executed ten months later.

In April 2003, the operational commander of the attack was Abd al Rahim al Nashiri, who had previously assisted one of the East Africa embassy bombers. He had arrived in Yemen in late 1999 to supervise the purchase of the boat used in the attack, and to direct the casing and executions of the attacks. Nashiri was assisted by an al-Qaeda member close to bin Laden, Tawfiq bin Attash (Khalid) who supplied the explosives used in the attack. The attack followed the operational pattern demonstrated in the East African embassy bombings—it was directed by key al-Qaeda operatives, using equipment and explosives purchased with al-Qaeda funds, and executed by members of al-Qaeda. By mid-November 2000, US investigators were aware of the roles Nashiri and Khalid had played in the attack, and that they were senior al-Qaeda operatives. The one part that could not be ascertained at the time was whether the attack had been carried out under direct orders from bin Laden himself. This could not be confirmed until Nashiri and Khalid were captured in November 2002 and April 2003 respectively.[68]

In retaliation for the bombing of the embassies in Africa and the USS Cole, the US President Bill Clinton ordered a missile strike on three Bin Laden camps in Afghanistan and a pharmaceutical plant in Sudan. The cruise missiles hit the al-Qaeda training camps and killed 26 Afghan Arabs though the real target had been Bin Laden and his deputies. The attack on the pharmaceutical plant however was seen as a blunder and an attempt by Bill Clinton to divert attention from his personal problems relating to the Monica Lewinsky affair.[68] This in turn diluted the public support for decisive measures in Afghanistan including possibly, the use of US ground forces to hunt down the terrorists.

The US response after the East Africa attacks did not intimidate the terror groups. In fact, two disrupted millennium plots demonstrated that al-Qaeda remained willing to provide support to attacks initiated by more independent actors. Neither intended Millennium attack was a traditional al-Qaeda operation: rather, both were planned and orchestrated by independent extremist groups which received training and assistance from al-Qaeda. One was a plot to destroy hotels and tourist sites in Amman, Jordan. It was planned and carried out by a Palestinian. The other was the attempted bombing of the Los Angeles International airport. It was orchestrated by Ahmed Ressam, who conceived and prepared for the attack on his own. Both Ressam and the Jordanian cell took what they needed from al-Qaeda—associated camps and personnel, but did not follow the traditional al-Qaeda top-down planning and approval model.[68]

Al-Qaeda Training Camps in Afghanistan

Many of the operatives in the African Embassy and the Cole attacks attended training camps in Afghanistan. The training at al-Qaeda and associated camps was multifaceted in nature. A worldwide operation needed operatives and also foot soldiers for the Taliban in its war against the Northern Alliance and guerrillas who could shoot down helicopters of invading armies in Afghanistan or Chechnya. Thus, most recruits received training that was geared towards conventional warfare. Terrorist training was provided mostly to the best and ardent recruits.[69]

The quality of training provided at al-Qaeda and other associated camps, was apparently quite good. There was coordination with regard to curriculum, and great emphasis on ideological and religious indoctrination. Instruction underscored that the United States and Israel were evil, and the rulers of Arab countries were illegitimate. Trainees in the camps did not focus solely on terrorist operations. Al-Qaeda instructors portrayed 'martyrdom' in the service of jihad as a noble act, and many recruits were eager to go on suicide missions.[68] As time passed and al-Qaeda repeatedly and successfully hit US targets, bin Laden became a legendary figure both in Afghanistan. He lectured at the camps. His stature and charisma reinforced the zeal of the trainees. Bin Laden also personally evaluated trainees' suitability for terrorist operations. The camps were able to operate only because of the worldwide network of recruiters, travel facilitators and document forgers who vetted would be trainees and helped them get in and out of Afghanistan. According to a conservative estimate thousands of men, perhaps as many as 20,000 trained in al-Qaeda supported camps between Bin Laden's return to Afghanistan in May 1996 and 11 September 2001.[69]

After establishing itself in Afghanistan, al-Qaeda relied on well placed financial facilitators and diversion of funds from Islamic charities. The financial facilitators raised money from donors in the Gulf countries and particularly in Saudi Arabia. The facilitators also appeared to rely heavily on certain imams at mosques, also primarily in the Gulf countries, who were willing to divert mandatory charitable donations known as 'zakat.' There is no convincing evidence that any government financially supported al-Qaeda before 9/11 (other than the limited support by the Taliban after bin Laden first arrived in Afghanistan).[71] Some governments may have turned a blind eye to al-Qaeda's fund raising activities. Saudi Arabia has long been considered the primary source of al-Qaeda funding, but there is no evidence that the Saudi government as an institution or senior officials within the Saudi government funded al-Qaeda. Still, al-Qaeda found fertile fund raising ground in the Kingdom, where extreme religious views are common and charitable giving is essential to the culture and, until recently, subject to a very limited oversight.[71] The United States has never been a primary source of al-Qaeda funding, although some funds raised in the United States may have made their way to al-Qaeda. No persuasive evidence exists that al-Qaeda relied on the drug trade as an important source of revenue, or funded itself through trafficking in diamonds from African states engaged in civil wars.[71]

After raising money, al-Qaeda frequently moved its money by "Hawala," an informal and ancient trust based system for transferring funds.[71] Al-Qaeda also used couriers as a secure albeit slower, way to move funds. Bin Laden relied on the established Hawala networks operating in Pakistan, the United Arab Emirates, and throughout the Middle East to transfer funds efficiently. Hawaladars (people connected with the Hawala) associated with al-Qaeda may have used banks to move and store money, as did various al-Qaeda fund raisers and operatives outside Afghanistan, but there is little evidence that bin Laden or his core al-Qaeda members used banks during this period. Al-Qaeda's money was distributed as quickly as it was raised—what was made was spent. The CIA estimates that al-Qaeda spent $30 million annually, including paying for operations, maintaining training camps, paying salaries to operatives, contributing to the Taliban and contributing to related organizations. The largest expense was payments to the Taliban, which totaled an estimated $10 to $20 million per year. Actual operations were relatively cheap. Although there is evidence that al-Qaeda experienced shortfalls as part of the cyclical fundraising process (with more money coming in the holy month of Ramazan).[72]

Operation Enduring Freedom

Throughout most of the twentieth century, the US armed forces were seen as a giant, able to win wars through brute force but often lacking in daring and cleverness. This basic strategy worked during the two world wars, making the United States relatively tough to challenge. But it failed in Vietnam, produced mediocre results in Korea, and worked in the Persian Gulf War as the terrain was ideally suited to American strengths. What a difference a new century makes. Operation Enduring Freedom has been, for the most part, a masterpiece of military creativity and finesse.[75] The Americans devised a plan for using limited but well-chosen types of military power in conjunction with the Afghan opposition to defeat the Taliban and al-Qaeda. They also persuaded Pakistan to sever its ties with Taliban, work with Afghanistan's Northern Alliance, provide the bases and over flight rights needed by the US forces, and contribute to the general war effort. The US success in defeating the Taliban deprived al-Qaeda of its sanctuary in Afghanistan and left its surviving leaders running for their lives. If the US strategy has had many virtues, it has also had flaws. Most important it has failed to achieve a key war goal: capturing or killing

Osama bin Laden and other top leaders of al-Qaeda. Such hunts are inherently difficult, but the prospects for success in this case were reduced considerably by US reliance on Afghan militias for sealing off escape routes and conducting cave to cave searches during critical periods.[75] But on balance, Operation Enduring Freedom has been very impressive. Beginning on 7 October 2001, Afghans, Americans and coalition partners cooperated to produce a remarkable victory in Afghanistan. The winning elements included 15,000 Northern Alliance fighters, primarily from Tajik and Uzbek ethnic groups. Hundred combat sorties a day by US planes, 300-500 Western special operations forces and intelligence operatives, a few thousand Western ground forces, and thousands of Pashtun soldiers in southern Afghanistan who came over to the winning side in November. Together they defeated the Taliban forces, estimated at 50,000 to 60,000 strong, as well as a few thousand al-Qaeda fighters.[71]

The short war had several phases. The first began on 7 October 2001, and lasted a month; the second ran through November and saw the Taliban lose control of the country; the third was characterized by intensive bombing of suspected al-Qaeda strongholds in the Tora Bora Mountain and cave complex in December; the fourth began with the inauguration of Hamid Karzai as President and continues to date.[74] During the first part of the war, Taliban forces lost their large physical assets such as radar, aircraft, and command and control systems, but they hung on to power in most regions. Most al-Qaeda training camps and headquarters were also destroyed. Although Taliban forces did not quickly collapse, they were increasingly isolated in pockets near the major cities. Cut off from each other physically, they were unable to re-supply or reinforce and had problems communicating effectively. Most air attacks occurred around Afghanistan's perimeter, because the rugged central highlands were not a major operating area for the Taliban or al-Qaeda. By the middle of October, most fixed assets worth striking had already been hit, so combat sorties turned to targeting Taliban and al-Qaeda forces in the field. Aircraft continued to fly at an altitude of at least 10,000 feet, because the Pentagon was fearful of anti-aircraft artillery, Soviet SA-7 and SA-13 portable anti-aircraft missiles and some 200-300 Stinger anti-aircraft missiles presumed to be in Taliban or al-Qaeda possession. But most precision guided weapons are equally effective regardless of their origin, provided good targeting information is available. The first month of the war produced only limited results and had many defense and strategic analysts worried about the basic course of the campaign.[74] Some of these critics called for a ground invasion; others opposed an invasion but thought a substantial intensification of efforts was necessary. In phase two beginning in early November, that intensification occurred. But it was not so much to an increased number of airplanes as to an increase in their effectiveness. By then, 80 percent of US combat sorties could be devoted to directly supporting opposition forces in the field; by late November the tally was 90 per cent. In addition, the deployment of more unmanned aerial vehicles and Joint Surveillance and Target Attack Radar System (JSTARS) aircraft to the region helped the United States maintain continuous reconnaissance of Taliban forces in many places.

Most important, the number of US special operations forces and CIA teams working with the various opposition elements increased greatly. As a result, Taliban and al-Qaeda collapsed in northern cities such as Mazar-i-Sharif and Taloqan over the weekend of November 9-11. Kabul fell soon afterwards. By 16 November, the Taliban controlled less than one-third[74] of the country, in contrast to 85 percent just a week before. Meanwhile, some Pashtun tribes had begun to oppose the Taliban. By November, they were accepting the help of US special-forces; two groups in particular—one led by Hamid Karzai, the other by another tribal leader, Gul Agha Shirazi-closed in on Kandahar. Mullah Omar fled with most of his fighters, leaving the city open by December 8-9. Pockets of Taliban and al-Qaeda resistance, each with hundreds of fighters or more, remained in areas near Mazar-e-Sharif, Kabul, Kandahar and possibly elsewhere, but the Taliban no longer held cities or major transportation routes.

Why this part of the campaign achieved such a rapid and radical victory remains unclear?[75] Taliban forces presumably could have held out longer if they had hunkered down in the cities and put weapons near mosques, hospitals and homes, making their arsenal hard to attack from the air. Opposition forces were too few to defeat them in street to street fighting in most places, and starving out the Taliban would have required the unthinkable tactic of starving local civilian populations as well. Most likely, the Taliban got caught in positions outside major cities that they could neither easily escape nor defend. Once the Afghan opposition began to engage the enemy seriously in November and Taliban returned fire, they revealed their positions to American special operations personnel who could call in devastating air strikes.

Sometimes, they were tricked into revealing their location over radio. Even trench lines were poor defenses against 2-ton bombs delivered within

10 to15 meters of their target. Just what Taliban fighters could have done differently, once stranded in the open terrain, is unclear. They might have been advised to go on the offensive or try to escape back into urban settings under cover of night or poor weather, although many US reconnaissance assets work well under these conditions. But both approaches would have been difficult and dangerous, especially for a relatively unsophisticated military force such as the Taliban. The third main phase of the war began in early December. By this time, US intelligence had finally pinpointed much of al-Qaeda's strength near Jalalabad, in eastern Afghanistan. In particular, al-Qaeda forces, including Osama bin Laden, were supposedly holed up in the mountain redoubts of Tora Bora. Travelling with perhaps 1000 to 2000 foreign fighters, most of them fellow Arabs, bin Laden could not easily evade detection from curious eyes even if he might elude US overhead reconnaissance.[75] Thus, once Afghan opposition fighters, together with CIA and special operations forces were deployed in the vicinity, US air strikes against the caves could become quite effective. By mid-December the fight for Tora Bora was over. Most significant cave openings were destroyed and virtually all signs of live al-Qaeda fighters disappeared and bombing virtually ended by late 2001.

So why did bin Laden and other top al-Qaeda leaders get away? The United States relied too much on its allies to close off possible escape routes from the Tora Bora region. The Afghans and the Pakistanis did not have the same incentives as the United States to conduct the effort with dogged persistence. Moreover the mission was inherently difficult. By mid-December, the Pentagon felt considerably less sure than it had been of the likely whereabouts of bin-Laden. Although estimates remain rough, Taliban losses in the war were considerable. According to New York Times correspondent Nicholas Kristoff, as many as 8,000 to 12,000 were killed—roughly 20 percent of the Taliban's initial fighting capability.[75] Assuming conservatively at least two wounded for every person killed, Taliban losses could have represented half their initial fighting strength, a point at which most armies have traditionally started to crumble. Another 7000 or more were taken prisoner. US forces lost about 30 personnel by the middle of March 2002. Most were Marine Corps and Army troops, but other personnel were lost as well.[75]

On the whole, Operation Enduring Freedom has been a success in both design and execution.[74] Using specially equipped CIA teams and special operations forces in tandem with precision-strike aircraft allowed for accurate and effective bombing of al-Qaeda positions. US personnel also contributed immensely to helping the Northern Alliance tactically and logistically. By early November, the strategy had produced mass Taliban retreats in the north of the country; it had probably caused many Taliban casualties as well. Most notably, the US effort helped quickly galvanize Pashtun forces to organize and fight effectively against the Taliban in the south, which many analysts had considered a highly risky proposition and CENTCOM had itself considered far from certain. Had these Pashtun forces decided that they feared the Northern Alliance and the United States more than the Taliban, Afghanistan might have become effectively partitioned, with al-Qaeda taking refuge exclusively in the south and the war effort rendered largely futile. Convincing these Pashtun to change sides and fight against the Taliban required the right mix of diplomacy, military momentum and finesse. Yet despite the overall accomplishments, mistakes were made.

The Pentagon's handling of al-Qaeda and Taliban detainees at Guantanamo Bay, Cuba, was one of them.[74] Whether these men should have been designated as prisoners of war can be debated. The POW issue aside, the administrations initial reluctance to guarantee the basic protections of the Geneva conventions to Taliban soldiers and its continued refusal to apply them to al-Qaeda were unwise. These decisions fostered the impression that the detainees were not being treated humanely. This perception became prevalent throughout the world and America's image in the Arab and Muslim world took a hit. The big US mistake, however, concerned the hunt for top al-Qaeda leaders. Rather than relying on Afghan forces to do the job in December near Tora Bora, the US army should have tried to prevent al-Qaeda fighters from fleeing into Pakistan by deploying American forces on or near the border. Admittedly, there were good reasons not to put many Americans in Afghanistan. First, Washington feared a possible anti-American backlash. Complicating matters, the United States would have had a hard time getting tens of thousands of troops into Afghanistan, since no neighbouring country except Pakistan would have been a viable staging base—and Pakistan was not willing to play that role.[77] But even though the reasoning was correct in general, it was wrong for Tora Bora. Putting several thousand US forces in that mountainous, inland region would have been difficult and dangerous. Yet given the enormity of the stakes in this war, it would have been appropriate. Indeed, CENTCOM made preparations for doing so.

But in the end, partly because of logistic challenges but perhaps also because of Pentagon's aversion to casualties, the idea was dropped. Furthermore, local US allies were not up to the job in Tora Bora.[75] They were not always fully committed to the mission and there were too few well equipped troops to prevent al-Qaeda and Taliban fighters from outflanking them.

Since the September 11 attacks, the defeat of the Taliban and lastly the killing of Osama bin Laden in May 2011, al-Qaeda's funding has decreased significantly. The arrests or deaths of other important financial facilitators have decreased the amount of money al-Qaeda has raised and increased the costs and difficulty of raising and moving that money. Some charities are now out of business, with many of their principals killed or captured, although some charities may still be providing support to al-Qaeda. Moreover, it appears that the al-Qaeda attacks within Saudi Arabia have reduced—perhaps drastically—al-Qaeda's ability to raise funds from Saudi sources. Both an increase in Saudi enforcement and a more negative perception of al-Qaeda by potential donors have cut its income.[75]

At the same time al-Qaeda's expenditures have decreased as well, largely because it no longer provides substantial funding to the Taliban or runs a network of training camps in Afghanistan. Prior to 9/11 al-Qaeda was a centralized organization which used Afghanistan as a war room to strategize, plan attacks, and dispatch operatives worldwide. Bin Laden approved all al-Qaeda operations, often selecting the targets and operatives. After al-Qaeda lost Afghanistan post 9/11, it fundamentally changed. The organization is far more decentralized as attested by the death of Osama bin laden in Pakistan on 2 May 2011 in a raid by the US forces, which barely caused a ripple. Even before his death, his seclusion had forced operational commanders and cell leaders to assume greater authority. As a result, al-Qaeda today is far more loose collection of regional networks with a greatly weakened central organization.[79]

4

AFGHANISTAN'S ETHNIC CONUNDRUM

In late 2001, when the US forces expelled the Taliban from Afghanistan, the country appeared headed for a breakup.[81] The United States and the rest of the international community feared the Afghanistan's rival ethnic groups would use their regional power bases to pull apart any unitary state, forming in its place independent mini- states or aligning with their ethnic brothers across Afghanistan's borders.[82] At that time, such fears seemed credible: NATO troops were still dealing with the fallout from the violent disintegration of former Yugoslavia in the 1990s.

The Afghans themselves, however, were less concerned about their country dividing. After all, Afghanistan has been a single state for more than 250 years.[77] If the country was going to split it would have done so in the 1990s, during its protracted civil war. Yet it did not. No Afghan leader of any political stripe or ethnicity endorsed succession at any time during the last century. Although Afghanistan's various factions disagreed about how the country's new government should be organized and would wield power within it, they all proclaimed support for a unitary state.[77]

A decade later, the anxiety of Washington and its allies has reversed itself. If in 2001 the West was afraid that the absence of a strong centralized government would prompt Afghanistan's dissolution, by 2011 the West has come to fear that dysfunctional centralized government could cause this same outcome. The government in Kabul has been undermined by the country's fraudulent 2009 presidential election, the absence of political parties, poor security and general corruption.[77]

Afghanistan's population of approximately 30 million people is divided into seven major ethnic groups—the Pashtuns, the Tajiks, the Hazaras, the Uzbeks, the Aimaqs, the Turkmens and the Baluchis—and many smaller ones. Although the Pashtuns claim to be the national majority, most analysts believe they constitute a plurality of between 40 and 45 per cent.[82] However, each ethnic group constitutes the majority in one or more of Afghanistan's regions: Pashtuns in the south and the east, Tajiks in the northeast and west, Hazaras in the center and Uzbeks in the northwest. On the political level, ethnicity in Afghanistan is more descriptive than operational, as most individual's primary loyalty is local—to kin, village, valley or region. There is little cohesiveness in large ethnic groups except when faced with an enemy ethnic group. Meanwhile, crosscutting ties of intermarriage, bilingualism, and political alliance regularly transcend ethnicity. Among non-Pashtuns, shared location is even more important: different ethnic communities in the same towns and villages often display more solidarity with one another than they do with their ethnic compatriots from other parts of the country. Ethnicity in Afghanistan consequently, is essentially pre-nationalist, with ethnic groups holding similar economic and political interests but no common ideology or separatist aspirations. Moreover the multi-ethnic state had long been the accepted norm in Afghanistan; it was not some anomaly that needed rectification. Ethnic conflicts in Afghanistan historically centered on which groups would dominate the state and subordinate others, not over which group would have exclusive control over territory.

As described in the earlier chapters, for most of the time between the sixth century BC, when the Persian Empire was founded, and the mid-eighteenth century, Afghanistan was divided among empires based in Central Asia, India and Iran.[5] These Turkish and Persian ruling dynasties taxed and administered each region's cities, trade routes and most productive agricultural areas. They won support by tying themselves to local elites who became junior partners in government. These regimes ignored the poor mountainous and desert regions, since they would not repay the cost of administration, until they caused trouble. The proud boast that Afghanistan has never been conquered is true only for these remote regions, not its cities or productive lands. In 1747, a Pashtun dynasty founded by Ahmad Shah Durrani took control of Afghanistan for the first time,[4] but Durrani followed the same pattern as his Turkish and Persian predecessors. Rulers in Kabul appointed governors (often their relatives) to regional cities but let them remain largely autonomous.

This pattern changed when Abdur Rahman Khan came to the throne in 1880.[37] Later known as iron Amir, Rahman aimed to rule Afghanistan directly without relying on intermediaries. Before finally subduing the country in 1895, his regime put down more than 40 uprisings and killed more than 100,000 people.[8] He ended the regional political autonomy that had formerly characterized Afghanistan and concentrated all political power in Kabul. The Pashtuns became Afghanistan's politically privileged group, although the Tajiks ran the government's administration. Uzbek, Aimaq and Turkmen disappeared from public life, even in their home regions; the Hazaras, meanwhile, faced active discrimination. Although all succeeding Afghan regimes emulated Rahman's centralized state, it proved hard to maintain.[37] In the century following Rahman's death in 1901, every one of Afghanistan's rulers either died violently or was driven into exile.

Although ethnic conflict played a role in Afghan politics in the twentieth century, it was never the reason for state collapse. Instead, it was ideology that brought down most regimes.[4] The country was cleaved by unresolved conflict between modernizing elites in Kabul and the more conservative rural inhabitants. The modernizers assumed they could change Afghanistan by decree, but they under estimated the military strength and administrative capability required to accomplish such a task. This conflict first proved fatal in 1929, when the reform minded Amanullah Khan[60] was overthrown by rural revolts within months of demanding sweeping social and legal changes. Two generations later in 1978, the same conflict arose when the Democratic Party of Afghanistan promulgated radical new social and economic policies that alienated rural Afghans.[70] Only the Soviet invasion the next year and a protracted occupation would keep the PDPA in power.

These conflicts did not pit different ethnic groups against one another: Pashtun Kings and Communists opposed rural Pashtun mullahs and tribal khans; a progressive Persian speaking intelligentsia in Kabul opposed conservative Persian speaking villagers. In both 1929 and 1978, insurgents allied across ethnic and regional lines, citing the common threat to their traditional ways of life and interpretations of Islam.[3] However, in the current insurgency in Afghanistan which reflects similar cultural and ideological fault lines, the Taliban have found it difficult to transcend their rural Pashtun ethnic base. In Afghanistan, such ideological conflicts are associated with opposition to established regimes, whereas ethnic and regional conflicts emerge in the vacuum of a state collapse.[82] Despite the decade that has elapsed since Taliban were driven from power, Afghanistan, at least politically, still remains in the post collapse era of uncertainty. Therefore, frustrating the Taliban insurgency is less about confronting the Taliban's ideology, which was never really popular in Afghanistan, than it is about creating a legitimate and a more stable Afghan state.[8]

If insurgencies topple established Afghan governments, their stable replacements emerge from the crucible of civil war. Rural rebels may stay united long enough to bring down governments in Kabul but lack enough cohesion to bring stable regimes of their own. When faced with a common threat or united in a common goal, such groups readily set aside the disputes that ordinarily divide them, only to rediscover them once the goal has been achieved. The Mujahideen insurgency against the PDPA that began in 1979 and the civil war that followed that regime's collapse in 1992 matched this pattern. The Mujahideen rallied nationwide opposition to the decade long Soviet invasion of Afghanistan. When the Soviets withdrew in 1989, however, unity among the Mujahideen began to fray. Those factions that had aimed to expel the Soviets saw little point in continuing the fight against Najibullah then the leader of the PDPA. He had already jettisoned the regime's radical communist ideology and now offered arms, money and local autonomy to those willing to leave the resistance.[91] This tactic succeeded well enough until the Soviet Union disintegrated in late 1991, taking with it outside military and financial support for the PDPA regime. Most former members of the PDPA then joined Mujahideen parties based on ethnic ties.

The Afghan civil war of the 1990s had no ideological foundation and pitted ethnic and regionally based factions against one another. With the exception of Abdul Rashid Dostum, the secular Uzbek militia leader, all other major factional leaders (Pashtun, Tajik Hazara) were Islamists of one variety or the other.[11] Although militia leaders mobilized members of their own ethic groups to fight, they fought not for the cause of an ethnic group but out of self-interest. Conflicts that appeared ethnic on the surface were in reality, fights over control of political, economic and military resources.[82]

If there was any overarching ethnic theme in the civil war in the 1990s, it was the attempt by non-Pashtuns to break the century old ethnic hierarchy that had discriminated against them. They demanded a return to an older pattern of regional autonomy, in which the local elites played a significant role in governing their own people and had a say in politics at the national level. The Pashtuns bridled at this suggestion of power but could do little to stop it. They were too divided and unable to unite behind a single Pashtun leader.[13] In the past they had always rallied around scions of the royal Durrani house, because both rural Pashtuns and non-Pashtuns accepted the legitimacy of such rulers. But in the 1990s, competing Pashtun Mujahideen leaders, such as Gulbadin Hikmatyar, vetoed this option, since each man wanted supreme power for himself. By 1994, in the absence of Pashtun unity, the civil war reached a stalemate: each faction could hold its own territory but was unable to move beyond it.[89]

The Taliban movement led by Mullah Omar and other low level Pashtun clerics from Kandahar broke this standoff. As Ibn Khaldun, the Arab social historian first noted seven centuries ago, religious leaders often prove more successful than tribal ones in uniting large groups in Islamic societies. Calling on God's authority, the Taliban circumvented clan rivalries and united the people In the name of religion. In theory, this dynamic should have given the Taliban nationwide appeal, but their leadership and membership remained too overwhelmingly Pashtun for this to happen. Although Taliban victories between 1995 and 1998 gave them control over most of Afghanistan's territory, non-Pashtuns resented the regimes heavy handed tactics and narrow ethnic chauvinism. They waited for an opportunity to turn against the regime. This moment, of course, would arrive in 2001, when the United States went to war against the Taliban in response to the 9/11 attacks. Within ten weeks of the beginning of the US military operations, the Taliban were expelled from Afghanistan. In the end, not even the Pashtuns in the Talban's home base of Kandahar proved willing to fight on their behalf.[74]

The fall of the Taliban left a power vacuum at the national level and restored clout to the regional leaders. But none of them opposed the formation of a new unitary government or sought to break away from it once it had been created. In the years and months that followed the US invasion, the discussions about Afghanistan's future and the architecture of its political system—the Bonn meetings, the 2002 national loya jirga (council of elders), and the 2003 constitutional convention—were marked more by cooperation than conflict. Equally significant was what did not happen: the non-Pastun Northern Alliance leaders, who had defeated the

Taliban, did not form a government unilaterally; except for some local score settling, the Pashtuns were not penalized for their earlier pro-Taliban sympathies; and no faction took on the role of a spoiler.[82] The agreement to make Karzai as the head of the government recognized the traditional Pashtun claim to executive power, but the ministries were divided among the different ethnic factions. Although many non-Pashtuns initially opposed Afghanistan's draft constitution because they wanted a less centralized government, the representatives ratified it unanimously, because no faction wanted to pick a fight. The new government's legitimacy would be judged by its effectiveness. Ironically, the major expected benefit of making Karzai, a Pashtun from Kandahar President, never materialized, because politics among rival clans in the south, divided the community between pro- and anti-Karzai factions to the benefit of the Taliban.[89]

The new government had an exceptionally strong executive, modeled on the constitution that ex King Zahir Shah's regime had written in 1964. Afghans in Kabul, many of whom had recently returned from abroad, had argued that this was necessary to prevent ethnic and regional division. They rejected alternate plans labeling those who favoured more regional autonomy and less presidential powers as tools of the "warlords" or ethnic blocs. The international community supported those Afghans in favour of centralization—although West's fears about ethnic destabilization reflected recent experiences in the Balkans more than Afghan reality.[13]

Like the US constitution, Afghan's new constitution made no mention of formal political parties and Karzai refused to allow candidates to run with any party affiliation or to let the parliament organize itself by party.[89] Karzai couched his opposition to political parties in the same rhetoric as Zahir Shah had used in the 1960s: parties lead to national discord. But his decision only reinforced non-political ties based on family, region or ethnic affiliation. For lack of alternatives, the Afghan parliament soon split into Pashtun and non-Pashtun blocs. Government ministries became ethnic enclaves, spoils that Karzai offered to ethnic leaders in exchange for their political support. At the same time, because Karzai made all appointments, even down to the sub-provincial level, palace patronage played a stronger role than democratic politics, in determining who governed at the local level. For regions that had grown accustomed to autonomy over the years, the arrival of Karzai's appointees, who abused their positions or favoured one faction over another, created hostility to the central government. When they reemerged in southern Afghanistan in 2005, the Taliban drew on this resentment and on the belief that Karzai did not represent a national Government so much as a family network keen to reward political allies and punish rivals.[93]

Afghanistan's various domestic problems have now become especially relevant for the United States and its allies as they look to withdrawing their forces over the next few years, with the goal of transferring the security responsibility to the Afghan government in 2014. A politically stable Afghanistan could accommodate a Taliban faction in government, whereas a politically unstable Afghanistan cannot. Ethnic perceptions will play a role in determining what kind of country will emerge as US and NATO forces begin to pull out.[82] At the moment, non-Pashtuns fear that Karzai will strike a deal with the Pashtun Taliban at their expense. They also believe that such a deal will not represent true power sharing but rather be a harbinger of Taliban's return. Instead of fighting another bloody civil war, as Afghanistan's non-Pashtuns did in the 1990s, they might instead abandon the unitary state and secede, leaving the Taliban to struggle for power, with other Pastun factions, in the south and east. Such a scenario will inevitable destabilize Pakistan's Pashtun majority regions, making the vast, ungoverned territories that border Afghanistan even more anarchic and a fertile ground for various terrorist groups.[90]

But it is not too late for the US to avoid this scenario. The United States should encourage the Afghan government to devolve power to provinces and districts so that the citizens there elect their own governors. Karzai currently makes all appointments, but such authority is not mentioned in the 2004 constitution and could thus be changed through legislation.[89] Opening up provincial and district governorships to competition would provide the safest form of power sharing with the Taliban. Whereas non-Pashtun Afghans oppose granting a role in the national government, they have few objections to the former and current Taliban members serving in districts or provinces where they have local support. Allowing the Taliban to serve in a democratic government, will likely lead to beneficial fissures within their ranks.

To achieve even these modest goals, the United States and its allies must address a question that is still dangerously taboo: the status of 2014 as a transition date in Afghan politics. According to the Afghan constitution, a President can serve only two consecutive terms, meaning that Karzai must relinquish his office when his second term ends in 2014. No Afghan ruler has stepped down voluntarily, however, Afghanistan is rife with speculation that Karzai intends to stay on regardless of the constitution.[89] Here, outside influence is especially important: most Afghans believe that without pressure from his patrons in the West, Karzai will not step down. Such moves by Washington and elsewhere need not be viewed as an attack on Karzai himself; after all this is a constitutional issue and not a personal one and Karzai has often argued that the Afghan constitution needs to be respected.[92] Even the inkling, that Kabul may have new leadership in 2014, would immediately open up Afghan politics to new ideas and personalities. If Washington leaves the question of executive powers unaddressed until 2014, then the much talked about transition of responsibility to the Afghan government may founder over disputes over the government's legitimacy. The best way then is to address these interests before conflict arises, not after it starts.[82]

5

Afghanistan Today

In the aftermath of 9/11, US forces achieved a rapid high tech victory over the Taliban government. Ten years later the Taliban are back. Fingers are pointing. The Europeans are too timid. The central government is weak. Pakistan is complicit. All that might be true. But the real problem grows out of how the United States defined its mission to begin with—that was to strike the Taliban but not get stuck in Afghanistan. The fact is that Afghanistan is a tribal country savaged by 30 years of war and further brutalized by the fundamentalist Taliban. Its infrastructure, educational system, agriculture—all was gone.[65] With the Taliban in retreat, traditional warlords re-established themselves. Vital political and economic assistance never arrived. Neither did a sufficiently strong international security force. Instead, a few thousand US troops were inserted to pursue the remnants of Taliban and al-Qaeda.[68]

The government of Hamid Karzai pieced together, was never able to extend its reach much outside Kabul. The results today are a mockery of early optimism. Despite the presence of over 140,000, US and NATO troops, security has worsened.[68] Opium has again become a major business. Infrastructure redevelopment lags, schools remain closed and across, great swathes of the country, the Taliban is resurgent. The real war however isn't military; it is political and economic. Destroying a few Taliban here and there does not provide what is essential—that is continuous security and the chance for political and economic redevelopment to take hold. Having squandered initial opportunities the Karzai government and its international backers now face a struggle against an indigenous guerilla force with substantial financial resources from opium production at home.[89] With the resurgent Taliban, all political and economic development is more difficult today than it would have been right after they were originally dispersed. NATO has supplemented US forces, but without demanding from the US a winning political and military strategy.[86]

The mission in Afghanistan at this time appears more distant and more difficult. The US is definitely not winning the war here. Instead it is at crossroads. If the US persists in failing to face up to the profound economic and political requirements of Afghanistan, if it neglects the need for strong coordination, if it thinks the mission is only about counter-terrorism or counter-drug production then it will surely loose. If the US does not take the right measures now the government in Kabul may well collapse and NATO will be severely damaged. This would have worldwide repercussions.[69]

How exactly did things get so bad so quickly? How did the fall of the Taliban—a great victory for Washington, and one that seemed to herald a new dawn for this battered country—lead to the return of the old status quo? The answer dates back to September 2001. Soon after al-Qaeda staged its attacks against New York City and Washington, from its Afghan bases, the Northern Alliance teamed up with the United States to rout the Taliban and their sponsors.[64] America's new allies, however, included some of the same men who had wreaked havoc in Afghanistan before Taliban came to power, and many of them were almost as radical in their ideology as the Taliban themselves (Rabbani, who was assassinated in 2011), while president from 1992 to 1996, granted more than 600 militant Arabs Afghan passports.[68] In addition, their alliance with Washington seems to have been tactical one at best. According to Milton Bearden who was the CIA's main liaison to the Mujahideen during the 1980s, 'they never thought they couldn't manage us'. Problems began even before the negotiation of the Bonn accord, signed in December 2001 under the UN auspices.

That agreement was supposed to serve as a road map for post-Taliban Afghanistan, leading to the development of a new, stable, democratic nation. The parties agreed that two Loya Jirgas would be held, one to elect an interim president and cabinet, and one to pass a constitution and set a time line for national elections.[70] But in the horse trading for cabinet positions that accompanied the agreement, three top posts—were given to members of the Jamiat-e-Islami, an Islamist ethnic-Tajik faction of the Northern Alliance led by Rabbani.

The leaders of the Northern Alliance agreed to the appointment of Karzai, an ethnic Pashtun, as interim president, but only because he did not have a militia of his own.[90] In practice, this meant that Karzai can do little to impose his will on those who retain private armies. Karzai took office as a nationalist, a believer in Afghanistan for all Afghans, regardless of ethnicity. But few of his colleagues share this view. The new government is composed of militarily strong Tajik, Uzbek, and Hazara factions and a weak Pashtun majority, governed by exiles who have recently returned to Afghanistan after decades elsewhere—mostly in the United States.[82] The United States and the UN presumably thought that Karzai would get the strength he needed to rule Afghanistan from the ongoing presence of Western soldiers in the country, who sometimes serve to enforce his writ. Yet even as Washington claims to support Karzai, it has continued to rely on the independent warlords for helping and hunting down remnant units of the Taliban and al-Qaeda. This dual strategy has served only to strengthen the former Northern Alliance by giving it US supplied guns, money and prestige, while eroding Karzai's already weak central authority.[71]

Even in Kabul, the limits of Karzai's power and the perfidy of the warlords have become clear. The Bonn agreement set clear timetables for the decommissioning of private militias. Even before they disbanded, these armies were to withdraw from Kabul. The Bonn agreement was unequivocal on this point: the warlord's troops were supposed to be out of the city by the time the International Security Assistance Force (ISAF) deployed there in late December 2001. The warlords never planned to honour these agreements. However, on 11 November, two days before the Taliban fled town, when the warlord Sayyaf was asked by satellite telephone about US requests that his militia remain outside Kabul, he laughed and said, 'Our brothers will be there'.[64] Another warlord Fahim, who would later become defense minister, took a similar position. Shortly after the Taliban were routed, he was asked if whether he was going to remove his troops from Kabul before the peace keepers entered the city. His answer was an unequivocal no. Fahim's troops remain in Kabul to this day; US and UN envoys are still trying to get rid of them.[68]

It is little wonder, then, that Karzai's attempts to assert himself and reassure his subjects have had little impact. Although Karzai has said that ordinary Taliban and the country's Pashtun majority have nothing to fear from the new regime, the disproportionate influence still wielded by the Tajik-Uzbek-dominated Northern Alliance has spread throughout the country.[71] This has been exacerbated by the small size of the international force stationed in Afghanistan. Just who are the men Washington has turned to for governing Afghanistan? President Karzai has praised the Mujahideen as heroes for their part in the war against the Soviets in the 1980s. But that is not how the ordinary Afghans view them. According to them, the Mujahideen forfeited the title of heroes and assumed the mantle of criminals when they took Kabul in 1992 and turned their guns on each other and the surrounding civilians.[70] Today the killing is blamed almost entirely on Gulbadin Hikmatyar a warlord, who fled to Iran in 1996 and is now battling the central government, and who, between 1992 and 1996, rained rockets on Kabul in a bid for power. However, all the Afghans who lived through that period know that all factions share blame. It was Sayyaf not Hikmatyar, who once said Kabul should be razed (since everyone who stayed behind during the rule of the communists must be communist themselves). Sayyaf's men—as well as those of Ahmed Shah Masud and his deputy, Fahim—carried out merciless attacks on civilians during the early 1990s, earning a reputation for brutality.[69]

The Americans, for their part, seem to know who they are dealing with but do not seem bothered by their histories. The warlords have now ruled the country for over ten years, since operation 'Enduring Freedom' and Afghanistan seems to be degenerating into a sort of narco-state, which could spin out of control. Not only are the warlords complicit in drug-running and corruption, but according to Afghanistan's Human Rights Committee, they are also guilty of abusing and harassing the population. The warlords have stolen peoples' homes, arbitrarily arrested their enemies, and tortured them in private jails.[89]

Those who speak out against the Mujahideen do so at their peril. Sima Samar, the head of the committee and a former minister of women affairs, was threatened with death for daring to criticize the warlords. So was a man who publicly chastised them during the first Loya Jirga; in fact, he was so frightened that he and his family subsequently sought political asylum. At the second Loya Jirga in December 2003, one woman—Malalai Joya, a 25-year-old social worker from the deeply conservative southwest—went so far as to denounce the 'Mujahideen heroes' from the stage, lambasting them as criminals who had destroyed the country. 'They should be brought to national and international justice', she told the assembly. In response, the then chairman of the Loya Jirga, Sibghatullah Mojaddidi—himself a former Mujahideen fighter—threatened to have her thrown out of the tent, demanded she apologize (she refused, although others did on her behalf), and granted Sayyaf, 15 minutes to respond, during which he called people like Joya criminals and communists.[64] Amnesty International has claimed that she subsequently received death threats. The Mujahideen may have proved good at abusing their fellow citizens, but they have not done as well at accomplishing the goal Washington has set for them: capturing or killing al-Qaeda and Taliban holdouts. Even as the factional militias have wreaked havoc among the general population, the Taliban have started to recover and regroup specially in the south and east. For example, government officials and Afghan aid workers in southeastern Zabul Province report that 8 out of Zabul's 11 districts are now run largely by the Taliban. Meanwhile much of the intelligence that the warlords have supplied to Washington on the Taliban has proved faulty. The problem according to Bearden is that the United States is 'not clever enough to not be manipulated. The reality is that the West as a whole doesn't mean much to the warlords'. Bearden warns that the warlords and factional leaders may not be willing to cooperate with the United States for much longer, since they will soon have resources to strike out on their own. He explains 'with $2.6 billion plus in poppies and another couple of billion that come through in the regular smuggling world, they can well tell the US they don't need it anymore.'

The main victims of all this have been ordinary Afghans. The public has grown disappointed and disillusioned with the International community, which it increasingly blames for not delivering on the lofty promises that preceded the US attack on the Taliban. The West has even empowered their former persecutors. According to a Human Rights Watch report, the 'fears of many Afghans—stem not only from ongoing abuses, but also from the memory of abuses committed by current rulers when they were previously in power in the early 1990s, before the Taliban seized power'.[68] As one woman in the rural area explained, 'We are afraid because we remember the past'.

The International community also failed to make good on its aid commitments. CARE International, a global humanitarian organization, reports that Afghanistan received pledges of only $42 per person over the next five years. In contrast, an average of $250 per person was pledged to the citizens of Haiti, Bosnia, East Timor, Kosovo and Rwanda. Moreover, there are increasing signs that the damage being done to Afghanistan will not be easily remedied. The chance to co-opt and pacify the country's majority Pashtun population has been squandered thanks to US policies that treat them as the enemy and empower minority Tajiks and Uzbeks instead. Moreover, the general lawlessness of the country means aid organizations no longer dare send their international workers outside the capital. They are particularly wary of the south and east, which have become the most dangerous regions. After the initial collapse of the Taliban, for example, 16 international aid organizations started operating in the southeastern province of Zabul. Today only two remain. The new dilemma is that Washington has started using military forces to provide aid, which many development officials complain blurs the line between soldiers and aid workers. The United States says this is the only way to get aid to the insecure southern and eastern regions. But Pierre Kraehenbuehl, former director of operations for the International Committee of the Red Cross explains the problem with the following example: 'One day a military civil affairs officer goes into a village and talks to villagers about reconstruction, and the same week a humanitarian worker goes to the same village, talks to the villagers and offers humanitarian aid. To the villagers they are the same. They are both Western, driving white vehicles. Then a few days later there is a military operation and there are possibly victims among the civilians. How do the people of the village make the distinction between those who may have been used to collect intelligence for that intervention?' The United States now recognizes that it made a mistake by not moving into the south and the east to mollify the Pashtun population.[75] As a result, Washington has adopted an 'accelerated' program aimed at providing big, highly visible reconstruction projects through provincial reconstruction teams (PRTS), run by the Defense Department with cooperation from some civilian agencies such as the US Agency for International Development and the State Department. Nine of these PRTS are currently at work, and several more are already starting up. The British now run a PRT in northern Mazar-Sharif, the Germans under NATO auspices in Northern Kunduz and the New Zealanders in central Bammiyan; the Americans are working through the troubled Pashtun dominated south and east.[74]

The PRTS are composed of a 'large number of military folk', according to Joseph Collins, former deputy assistant secretary of defense for stability operations. Collins says that using the military to do aid work is 'inevitable' in a dangerous environment like Afghanistan's. But although aid workers agree that Afghanistan is dangerous, they disagree with Washington about how soldiers should be used to address this. According to Kevin Henry, former advocacy director for care International, Western forces should not provide aid directly but instead should create a more secure environment by arresting the warlords and helping to train the national police and the army. This would allow aid organizations to return to the afflicted regions and do the kind of work they are best at. Despite the overarching insecurity and instability throughout Afghanistan, there have been a few limited successes. For example, a new Kabul to Kandahar highway opened in December 2003. Originally slated for completion in 2005, the project was sped up, reportedly by order of the White House. Such projects are hugely expensive, however. The highway cost $250 million, or roughly $625,000 per kilometer, since entire asphalt plants had to be airlifted into the region. Yet plans have been announced to build another 1,400 kilometers of highway and secondary roads, many of them in the neglected south and east. International donors, led by the United States, have also announced plans to build a large hydroelectric dam, as well as new schools, courthouses, and administrative buildings. Given the sorry reality of Afghanistan today—with its flourishing drug trade, widespread insecurity, sluggish disarmament, and insufficient international aid—such projects will not be enough to stabilize the country. If Washington really wants to help, it must abandon its policy of working with the warlords and factional leaders of the Northern alliance. These Northern Alliance warlords and their men have nothing to offer Afghanistan that would help the country move forward. Concessions made to the warlords will be met with demands for more concessions.[81] Instead, the United States should concentrate on training a police force, which, along with the national army that the United States and France are helping to build, could provide security at a local level. Unfortunately, the United States shows no sign of abandoning its warlord allies. In fact Khalizad the former US ambassador, has suggested that the local militias—the same groups that the U.N. is trying to disarm and reintegrate into Afghan society—be used to provide security. Khalizad has said that these men could be vetted and paired with US Special Forces. But this would be like using foxes to guard a hen house.[86] Moreover, the militias have worked with Special Forces for four years now and have shown no sign of improving their behaviour. On the contrary, they have focused much of their efforts on drugs, extortion and intimidation, using their relationship with US soldiers to frighten local civilians and advance their own greed. Washington's willingness to using these men suggests that the US policy makers have learned little from the last four years. Vikram Parekh, senior analyst at the International Crisis Group, calls US policy in Afghanistan 'an improvised political strategy essentially designed to give an appearance of stability in Afghanistan'. He says the United States and the UN are following a 'checklist strategy', achieving minor benchmarks without doing much to make Afghanistan stable in the long run. In the November 2004 and again in 2009 elections, Karzai was elected to five year terms, with significant powers under the new constitution to build strong institutions, including a national army and a police force.[89] To date, the hopes and the aspirations of the Afghan people have not been realized. Karzai has proved a weak and an ineffective ruler. He has been unable to deal with the rampant corruption, thriving drug trade (bigger today than at any time in Afghanistan's past), general lawlessness and insecurity, and dangerous private militias. The new army which totals no more than 80,000 soldiers is losing recruits almost as quickly as it can acquire them and the police force is still in its infancy.

Yet much more international help seems unlikely. With a disenchanted public who are tired of the demands of the two wars on the economy, it seems improbable that the United States will offer to play a larger role in Afghanistan for much longer and has even announced the deadline of 2014, for withdrawal of troops from the country. Until that date, even without a huge new investment, Washington could help matters by making a few key changes. To begin with, it should improve coordination with its European allies in Afghanistan. Here American lead is key, since hardly any other NATO countries have been willing to send more than a few hundred troops to the country, and those they have on the ground, remain in the big cities, avoiding the troubled areas in Afghanistan's east. Within Afghanistan, the United States should recognize that it needs partners other than the Northern Alliance and former exiles. The warlords must be abandoned. Removing the warlords—perhaps by granting them ambassadorial or other posts outside the country—will weaken their followers and make disarmament much easier. Washington should also reach out to the majority of the population, especially the Pashtuns.[86] On the security front, the United States should focus its hunt on those leaders who collaborated with al-Qaeda. The rank and file of Taliban, however, should not be ostracized. As for narcotics which, has now become Afghanistan's biggest problem, the United States and the Karzai government should consider how the Taliban managed to reduce this trade.[90] The Taliban, which banned all drugs in their final years, used a simple but effective strategy that could be replicated today: holding village elders and mullahs responsible for poppies grown in the area. Offenders were jailed for a month and their crops were burned. As a result, the village elders made sure to inspect their territories every morning before dawn (the best time for planting poppies) to make sure no illicit crops were being grown. If Washington decides to adopt these strategies, it has a chance of helping turn Afghanistan around—or at least of improving the current situation. If it turns its back on the country, however it will break faith with the Afghan people, who took the West at its word when it said it would not abandon them again.[74]

US Relations with Pakistan

Afghanistan has now been at war for three decades—a period longer than the one that started with World War I and ended with Normandy landings on D-day in World War II, and that war is now spreading to Pakistan and beyond.[81] This war and the attendant terrorism could spread to other continents—as on 9/11—or lead to the collapse of a nuclear armed state.

The Afghan and Pakistani security forces lack the numbers, skills, equipment and motivation to confront the insurgencies in the two countries or to uproot al-Qaeda and its associate, the Pakistani Taliban from their bases in the FATA along the Afghan-Pakistani border.[68] Proposals for improving the security situation focus on the additional 33,000 US troops sent to Afghanistan in 2010-11 to bolster the International forces, building larger national security forces in Afghanistan, and training and equipping Pakistan's security forces, which are organized for conflict with India, for domestic counter-insurgency. But none of these proposals is sufficient to meet the current, let alone the future threats.[81]

Unfortunately, no government in the region around Afghanistan supports a US or NATO presence there. Pakistan sees even the current deployment as strengthening an India allied regime in Kabul; Iran is concerned that the US will use Afghanistan as a base for launching regime change in Tehran and China, India and Russia all have reservations about a NATO base within their spheres of influence and believe they must balance threats by al-Qaeda and Taliban against those posed by the US and NATO.[83] Securing Afghanistan and its region will require an International presence for many years, but only a regional initiative that creates a consensus to place stabilizing of Afghanistan ahead of all other objectives, could make a long-term deployment possible.

Afghanistan needs larger and more effective security forces, but then it also needs revenue to sustain these forces. A decree signed by President Karzai in December 2002 would have capped the Afghan National army at 70,000 troops.[89] The former US Defense Secretary, Robert Gates then announced a plan to increase them to 122,000 and added 82,000 as police force bringing the total to 204,000. Current costs for sustaining such a force are $ 2.5 billion for the Army and $1.0 billion for the police force.[81] This would significantly exceed the current Afghan revenue of $ 670 million. In short, the army and the police alone would cost significantly more than Afghanistan's total revenue.

If Afghanistan cannot support its security forces at the currently proposed level on its own, even under the most optimistic economic scenario, a long-term international support or a long-term international presence is not viable, there is only one way that the ANSF (Afghan National Security Force) can approach sustainability: the conditions are changed so that Afghanistan no longer needs such large and expensive security force. Changing these conditions, however, will require changing the behaviour of actors not only inside but also outside of the country—which would mean putting more pressure on Pakistan to rein in the militants. Any additional pressure or putting boots on the ground in the tribal belt could have a negative impact, resulting in the alienation of the Pakistan military and the government. An adversarial Pakistan would further exacerbate the situation in Afghanistan, and make the situation increasingly dire.[92]

After the first phase of the war in Afghanistan ended with the overthrow of the Taliban in 2001, and the US prepared to invade Iraq, Washington's limited agenda in the region was to press the Pakistani military to go after al-Qaeda; meanwhile Washington ignored the broader insurgency, which remained marginal until 2005.[68] This suited the Pakistani military's strategy which was to assist the United States eliminate al-Qaeda but to retain the Taliban as a potential source of pressure on Afghanistan. But the summer of 2006 saw a major escalation of the insurgency, as Pakistan and the Taliban interpreted the United States decision to transfer command of coalition forces to NATO as a sign of intention to withdraw.[83] They also saw non-US troop contributors as more vulnerable to political pressure generated by casualties. The Pakistani military does not control the insurgency, but it can affect its intensity. Putting pressure on Pakistan to curb the militants will likely remain ineffective.[81] The region is rife with conspiracy theories trying to find a rational explanation for the United States supporting a major 'non-NATO ally' whose interests do not coincide with that of the US. Many believe that the United States is secretly supporting the Taliban as a way to keep the war going to justify its troop presence, which is actually aimed at securing the energy resources of Central Asia and countering China. Many in Pakistan believe that the US has deceived Pakistan into conniving with Washington to bring about its own destruction: India and the US supported Afghanistan will form a pincer around Pakistan to dismember the world's only Muslim nuclear power. More fundamentally, the concept of 'pressuring' Pakistan is flawed. No state can be successfully pressured into acts it considers suicidal.[81] The Pakistani security establishment believes that it faces both a US–Indian–Afghan alliance and a separate Iranian–Russian alliance, each aimed at undermining Pakistani influence in Afghanistan and even dismembering the Pakistani state. Some in the establishment see armed militants within Pakistan as a threat—but they largely consider it one that is ultimately controllable, and in any case secondary to the threat posed by their nuclear armed enemies.[81]

Pakistan's military command, which makes and implements the country's national security policies, shares a commitment to a vision of Pakistan as a homeland for the South Asian Muslims, and therefore to the incorporation of Kashmir into Pakistan. It considers Afghanistan as within the security perimeter. Add to this that Pakistan does not have border agreements with either India, into which Islamabad contests the incorporation of Kashmir, or Afghanistan, which has never explicitly recognized the Durand line, which separates the two countries, as interstate border.[43]

The Death of Osama bin Laden

Bin Laden was killed on 2 May 2011 in a secret raid carried out by US commandos (Seals) on a compound located at stone's throw from the Pakistan Military Academy in Abbottabad. According to Hillary Clinton, the US Secretary of State, 'there is no evidence that any senior Pakistani official had any idea of Osama bin Laden's whereabouts.' Despite the fact that the al-Qaeda leader was living so close to Pakistan's premier military academy, 'We have no reason to believe that that anyone in the highest levels of the government knew,' so declared the US Secretary of State.[83] 'They were quite emotional, conveying that they would have gone after him if they had known he was there.' Nevertheless, she told reporters, Pakistani leaders did acknowledge that a viable support network had existed inside their country, admitting that someone, somewhere, was providing some kind of support to bin Laden.

Clinton and US Joint Chiefs of Staff Chairman Admiral Mike Mullen spoke at a joint press conference after meeting with Pakistan's top civilian and military leadership in order to sort out the troubled US–Pakistan security relationship. Both Clinton and Mullen made clear that Washington expects greater cooperation to help 'disrupt dismantle and defeat al-Qaeda and to drive them from Pakistan and the region' in the future. 'We look to the government of Pakistan to take decisive steps in the days ahead,' Clinton said. 'Joint action against al-Qaeda will make Pakistan and America and the world safer and more secure.'

Clinton did not specify just what those steps might be, but she had a list of other problems that need work. For one thing, the Afghan Taliban continue to travel freely to and from their bases inside Pakistan. "Pakistan has the responsibility to help us help Afghanistan by preventing the insurgents from reaching the war from Pakistani territory," she said. For another Pakistan seems to be playing a double game by seeking and accepting billions in US aid, while at the same time stoking anti-Americanism and wild conspiracy theories among the Pakistani public rather than tamping them down.[83]

Even as the Pakistani government and military secretly support US drone attacks in the tribal border lands, they publically denounce them as violation of Pakistan's sovereignty. The Pakistani public's anger is only compounded by their government's failure to debunk incessant rumors that America is trying to destabilize Pakistan and steal its nuclear weapons. "Pakistan should realize that anti-Americanism and conspiracy theories will not make their problems disappear," Clinton said. "Deliberate misunderstandings, conspiracy theories and accusations have nothing to do with how we chart our future."

"Pakistan has given too little credit for the roughly $20 billion in aid that has been delivered in the last ten years," Clinton said. "We have repeatedly delivered on what we have promised by providing what we have promised by providing billions of dollars in assistance," she said. "We provide much more support than Saudi Arabia, China and everyone else combined." Nevertheless, American aid alone will not solve the country's myriad problems of poverty, illiteracy, power shortages and terrorism. "America could not and should not solve Pakistan's problems," she said.[83]

But Clinton said the message she will take home will be to insist that more and not less, cooperation is needed to fight terrorism and to aid beleaguered Pakistan. "I return to Washington ever more committed to doing what I can to make sure the cooperation we are seeking from Pakistan is forthcoming and the cooperation we have been asked for by Pakistan, is also forthcoming. After all, Pakistan has done more in the fight against violent extremism than it generally gets credit for. As Pakistani officials often point out, their country has lost far more soldiers fighting as Qaeda and the Pakistani Taliban in the past few years than America has lost in a decade of combat in Afghanistan."

Admiral Mullen's comments were more cautious, emphasizing the serious trust deficit that divides the countries' armed forces. "I have no illusions about the difficulties ahead, nor do I leave misinformed about the trust that still needs to be rebuilt between our two militaries." Because of recent tensions between the two countries, Pakistan has sought a significant reduction in the number of US military personnel stationed in the country. "There have been requests to reduce these numbers," Mullen said. "We are working our way through how those numbers look in the future."[83]

But Washington has powerful motivation to mend its ties with Islamabad. As Mullen noted, Pakistan cooperation is essential if al-Qaeda is to be defeated. Although bin Laden's death has thrown al-Qaeda into "disarray" and "disrupted some of its future plans," the organization has not been eviscerated, Mullen said: "Bin Laden's death has not eliminated the threats we both face from terrorism. Nor has his death meant the death of al-Qaeda altogether. Al Qaeda's alliances with the elements of the Taliban remain intact," Mullen said. "We see that collusion still persists." Mullen expressed the hope that Pakistan army chief General Ashfaq Kayani intends to resolve the differences. "I do leave here with a sense that General Kayani and other military leaders share my commitment to that task and share my desire to look for ways to advance the relationship."[83]

PAK-US MARRIAGE

Doomed but not divorced The fraught relations between Pakistan and the US have often been likened to a bad marriage in which the two partners can't live with each other, but are bound together by mutual dependency.

The relationship has been further exacerbated by the NATO attack which took place on two Pakistani checkposts on 26 November 2011 in which 24 Pakistani soldiers were killed. In retaliation Pakistan halted all NATO supplies and put US on notice to vacate the Shamsi airbase in Baluchistan as well as refused to participate in the Bonn conference on Afghan security. All these actions underline the transactional nature of the Pakistan–US relationship: if you give this, we will give you that. And as a renter state, Pakistan has some valuable geopolitical real estate to offer.[87]

The reality is that there has never been a convergence of values or long-term interests between the two countries, despite their long and troubled alliance. True, both states started off by entering into anti-communist pacts in the 1950s. But for Pakistan, this was a way of acquiring American arms in its rivalry with India.

Once the USSR. imploded, the rental value of Pakistan fell to zero in US eyes. Military and economic sanctions to discourage nuclear proliferation kicked in, the supply of F-16 fighters which Pakistan had paid for was blocked and Pakistan was declared an international pariah when it tested its nuclear devices in 1998.[86]

Just as it seemed the relationship was doomed forever Osama bin Laden launched his war on America, and with 9/11 a second honeymoon began. But the lack of any solid basis to the partnership beyond short-term needs has meant that it is always going to be hostage to outbursts and spats that threaten to spiral out of control.

Ultimately, the relationship is resurrected each time it hits rock bottom because of the mutual need of the two countries. The Pakistani military desperately needs the high tech weaponry, it is unable to procure elsewhere and its economy can't do without the assistance that trickles in fitfully from Washington. More urgently Pakistan needs American support for the frequent requests it makes for multilateral aid.

American needs are more straightforward: Pakistan's approval for the use of its airspace to support NATO troops in Afghanistan, from aircraft carriers in the Arabian Sea, the use of Pakistan's road network to carry supplies overland and the interdiction of cross-border militancy.

It is this last task that has proved so contentious. Over the years, as the NATO casualties have mounted, Western leaders have blamed Pakistan for "not doing enough" to combat militants based on its soil, and for not stopping them from crossing into Afghanistan at will to fight NATO and Afghan forces.

Another is the Pakistan army's need to have proxies in place for the post-US scenario in Afghanistan in which the pre-9/11 civil war is likely to resume. The third lies in the inherent danger in taking on the Haqqani network at a time when the army has its hands full already fighting the local Taliban. And finally, there are problems inherent in repeatedly ordering the Pakistan's Frontier Corps to fire on fellow Muslims and fellow Pakhtuns. The Pakistan army is also unhappy at the charge that it is not doing what it was supposed to despite the billions it was getting from the Pentagon. The officer corps is angry at being thought of as a mercenary army, doing the bidding of foreigners for financial considerations. In its eyes, it has national interests to protect, irrespective of the military aid it is getting.

Clearly there is a mismatch of expectations here. For the American public, politicians and media, the narrative is about paying hard cash to buy certain services, and getting short changed. This is the nature of a transactional relationship: when the customer does not think he is getting what he has paid for, he complains loud and hard.

From the popular Pakistani perspective, it has already paid too high a price for entering into this war on America's side. In terms of lives lost as well as economic damage, the public perception—whipped up by populist media—is that enough is enough.[84]

According to an opinion poll, 55 per cent of all Americans consider Pakistan as an enemy. This bleak view of its alliance partner is similar to the perception of two-thirds of all Pakistanis about the US. So clearly there is not much warmth in the doomed marriage.

Nevertheless the joyless couple is condemned to carry on with a facade of a united front for the next three years when the US forces are scheduled to begin pulling out of the quagmire, Afghanistan has proved for them. This time though, there is little prospect of the couple getting back together.

From the American perspective, a combination of a slumping economy and 15 years of bad vibes will make any resumption of US aid politically impossible. As it is, there is an increasing resistance to military and economic assistance. Only the presence of US troops in the region is making it possible for the Obama administration to continue disbursing aid.

For many Pakistanis, this cut off will only reinforce the popular image of America—fed by years of propaganda—as a fickle fair-weather ally, who abandons its friends when they aren't needed.[85]

6

How Pakistan was Talibanized?

The current instability and unrest in Pakistan is directly linked to the political uncertainty in Afghanistan. While the abdication of King Zahir Shah followed by the assassination of President Sardar Daud, were a source of concern for the US, the Soviets were equally if not more perturbed by these developments.[64] That is why Afghanistan became a hotbed of conspiracies and revolutions which resulted in change of leadership in quick succession. The assassination of President Daud was followed by the killing of Presidents Nur Muhammad Taraki and Hafizullah Amin. The last but one Soviet sponsored President, Babrak Karmal, fled Afghanistan in 1989 to Moscow, where he died in obscurity in 1996.[68] The last Afghan President, Dr. Najibullah was captured by the Taliban from the UN compound, and hanged.

The forerunner of Islamic fundamentalism in Pakistan was the movement spearheaded by the religious parties in 1977 against the Bhutto regime.[86] It had the tacit support of the United States who was unhappy with Bhutto because of his flirtation with China and socialism. During his five year tenure he had nationalized Industries, Banking and Insurance which was not received well by the elites in the country. He also played to the Islamic gallery by staging an Islamic conference in which all the Muslim countries in the world were represented.[94] The Islamic movement eventually resulted in the toppling of the Bhutto government and a takeover by the army General Zia Ul Haq who was willing to go the extra mile to please America. He got rid of Bhutto by getting a pliant judiciary to pass a death sentence against him for ordering the murder of a political opponent. While the intended victim was unhurt, his father was killed in the attack. Consequently on 4 April 1979 Prime Minister Bhutto was hanged like a common criminal.[96]

At the same time, an Islamic revolution broke out in Iran in February 1979 spearheaded by a cleric Ayatollah Khomeni. This was a cause of deep concern to the US as after all, Iran had the third largest oil reserves in the world (after Saudi Arabia and Iraq). Also, the revolution displaced the Shah who was considered a bastion of pro-West and pro-American sentiment in the Middle East.[86] The revolution in contrast was avowedly anti-American and anti-West and could become a precursor to similar revolutions in other countries of the Middle East. The Americans were also concerned about the situation in Afghanistan, where leftist politicians with the support of the Soviets had taken control of the country. The Soviet plan to seek access to the warm waters of the Arabian Sea by first occupying Afghanistan followed by Baluchistan in Pakistan was well known to the leaders of both America and Pakistan. This had to be prevented at all costs. General Zia-ul-Haq with the support of the Americans, started dabbling in Afghan politics by establishing contacts with the rebel leaders, who were called the Mujahideens (freedom fighters).[43]

The first to be recruited was Gulbadin Hekmatyar who was the leader of the Jamat Islami in Afghanistan. A branch of the same party already existed in Pakistan. Hikmatyar received training and finances from the Pakistani intelligence service.[43] He returned to Kabul, where it is believed, he was responsible for bomb explosions in the city targeting his opponents. Soon thereafter, in December 1979, the Soviets invaded Afghanistan.

Zia-ul-Haq was immensely pleased with this development, as he now felt secure in his position as Head of State. The Soviet Invasion would deflect attention from his military dictatorship and would gain support from the US and other Western nations. He believed if Afghanistan could be freed from the Soviet yoke, it could one day provide strategic depth to Pakistan in any future conflict with India.[86] Even today there are many supporters of this concept which includes the former Director General of ISI, Hameed Gul.

The Republican Party won the General elections in 1980 and Ronald Reagan became the President Zia-ul-Haq was one of the first guests to be invited to the White House. The US committed military aid to Pakistan to the tune of $4 billion along with a promise to support an Islamic holy war against the Soviets.[86] This was the time when refugees from Afghanistan were pouring into Pakistan. A recruitment camp was set up by Pakistani and US military personnel to train the so called holy warriors to wage jihad against the Soviets. By 1984 these jihadi organizations numbered almost two dozen and were financed by the American CIA and the Pakistani ISI. Over a period of time, when some of the Jihadists got restive and demanded more money, the CIA started weeding them out and cut down their number to just seven. The others were either disbanded or merged.[68]

Pakistan too got into the act by contacting other Islamic countries for money and military support. Saudi Arabia was amongst the first to help financially and allowed Osama bin Laden to recruit thousands for fighting in Afghanistan. Islamabad had by then become a prominent base for the CIA. According to the American journalist, Bob Woodword,[72] the director of CIA William Casey would fly into Islamabad almost every month to discuss the progress of the Afghan jihad with General Zia-ul-Haq. The dilapidated capital of the North West Frontier Province (NWFP) in Pakistan, Peshawar, also had its field day. It became a Mecca for Arab and other jihadists from Islamic countries around the world. The flag bearers of this Jihad were Osama bin laden and Abdullah Azzam, beside many other Arabs who had pitched their tents in Peshawar and were recruiting Pakistani and Afghan fighters for fighting this war. Millions of dollars were collected in the name of religion and disbursed amongst the people to persuade them to join the holy war. One result of the congregation of these zealots as well as the money that poured in from Saudi Arabia was that the madrasas (religious schools) which had numbered about 5000 in 1973 now reached 20,000 by 1986.[86] Another impact of this war was on the organizations that were fighting war of liberation in Indian held Kashmir. They abandoned their fight and joined in this lucrative jihad by recruiting fighters from the Punjab, particularly from the poverty stricken southern Punjab. Over one hundred thousand fighters, local and foreign received training at the ISI managed centres in and around the Pakistan's tribal belt.[76]

As a result of the US support, 38 countries, Islamic and non-Islamic joined hands to face the Soviets in Afghanistan. While the support from Western Europe was restricted to money and good-will, the US went all the way, providing Pakistan with new weaponry as well as finances for the freedom fighters (Mujahideen).[69] The large multinational oil companies in the region also contributed generously. One interesting partner in this war was China, who despite its Communist ideology joined the West against the Soviets proving that national interests supersede ideologies and religious affiliations.[68] Another example was the relations between Iran and the US. After the revolution there was a wide chasm in their relations. But on the Afghanistan issue they became virtual allies despite the fact that Saudi Arabia, whose regime was hated by the Iranians, was also a US ally.[86] Thus Pakistan became a base camp for Jihadis from all over the Islamic world. There was little introspection on the consequences for Pakistan, when this holy war ended. The streets of Peshawar were crawling with fighters who were fired up with Islamic zeal and armed to the teeth with Kalashnikovs and other military items. The use of opium, smuggled in from Afghanistan, was rampant. The war in Afghanistan has now bequeathed to Pakistan a culture seethed in violence, drugs and smuggling. For example, In the 1980s the number of people using opium numbered only 5,000. By the year 2000 this number had mushroomed to 300,000. The question that nobody bothered to ask, least of all the Pakistani leaders was whether Pakistan can survive this cultural tsunami?[86] The huge influx of US dollars, drugs, military hardware and smuggling had opened the doors to another curse—corruption from which the country would never recover.[94]

By 1986, the US was spending around $600 million per annum for arms and ammunition alone. The Pakistani leaders were complacent and without a clue, as to who would be the next target of these gun totting jihadists, once the war was over. The answer would come almost two decades later when these zealots would turn on Pakistan in an orgy of blood and gore. The question being asked today is whether Pakistan an economically weak and a politically unstable nation remain intact within its current geographical boundaries?[80]

Besides the inept and corrupt leaders, the ethnically minded groups unfortunately continue to revel in their bloody mindedness, by supporting a jihadist agenda while a majority of the Pakistanis sit on the sidelines as silent spectators. Today the two Pakistani cities Peshawar and Quetta are centres of arms and drug smuggling. Every day there are bomb explosions throughout the country with links to these cities. New blood feuds and vendettas have sprouted which take a large toll of human life. To date, it is believed that 30,000 Pakistanis and 5000 military personnel have been killed, a fall out from the Afghan war.[81]

A total of 48 nations participated in the Afghan war.[86] They came from Africa, Middle East, South East Asia and Central Asia to Pakistan, some seeking martyrdom and others enticed by the glitter of US dollars and Saudi Riyals reminiscent of the gold rush in Alaska. Pakistan was gradually going through a metamorphosis becoming an intolerant society in the name of religion. Minor differences in ideologies were exploited and over 200 organizations were formed feeding on a religious frenzy.[97] Some sought their own fiefdoms while others dreamt of reviving the Islamic caliphate of the middle ages. America was tolerant and even supportive of these groups as long as they served the purpose of fighting their arch enemy, the Soviets. Little did the Americans realize that one day their 'experiment' would have dangerous consequences for America and the Western world in the shape of Osama bin Laden, Ayman Zawaheri, Mullah Omar and the Taliban. As a consequence, America would have to return to Afghanistan again, two decades later, in a continuation of the war but this time against their former protégés the Taliban.[86]

The Afghan war also benefitted the Pakistani Generals who extended their hold on power in the country and at the same time accumulated billions of dollars. They had hit a jackpot in the lottery. The Generals joined hands with the religious parties and other extremists who in return honored General Zia-ul-Haq with the title 'The Caliph of the Muslim Ummah.'[86] In support of his military dictatorship they declared that democracy was un-Islamic and that there was no place for political parties in Islam. Zia was pleased and now considered his rule as impregnable. After all he had contrived to obtain the unquestioned support of the US as well as the powerful religious clergy. The political parties were declared redundant. The General's brand of Islam became a tool to legalize his rule. He believed that the religion alone, and that too the Saudi brand of Islam, was the panacea for the country's divisive ethnic mindset. In pursuance of that goal, he established a 'Majlis e Shura' (council of elders) and also wanted to set up Sharia courts on the pattern of Saudi Arabia. To observe Saudi practices at close hand, he sent a delegation of young religious scholars to Saudi Arabia for training.[86]

The sad truth is that during the period 1980 to 1991, on both side of the Durand line, the training camps had become nurseries, spawning vicious religious extremists who would go on to become a poison for the whole civilized world and in the process besmirch the teachings of a great religion. This poison continues to permeate through the Afghan and Pakistani societies and those who dare to oppose them are ruthlessly eliminated. While the organizations that mentored these extremists battled each other in matters of self-interest, they were nonetheless, united in their diehard opposition to secular, progressive and democratic forces. The state under General Zia-ul-Haq joined these extremists in eliminating his political opponents, branding them un-Islamic. Pakistan was now well and truly on the way to becoming a fundamentalist state—a haven for future terrorist organizations.[96]

Before the Afghan war, the fundamentalist organizations were at loggerheads with each other on sectarian basis. They opposed each other through literature which was published and disseminated in the populations. The Afghan war and the opposition to the Soviets brought them together on a united platform. So when the Soviets retreated from Afghanistan and there was no longer a common enemy to contend with, these organizations turned their guns and attention towards Kabul and against each other. The extremists in Pakistan also began their jihad, this time against minority Muslim sects.[86] The first target was the Shia community. These extremist organizations, after their Jihad in Afghanistan, were flush with money and arms and therefore had no problems in taking on anyone. As a reaction Shia militant organizations, with the support of Iran, came into existence. The stage was now set in Pakistan to enforce the law of the jungle.

After the retreat of the Soviets the warlords took control of Afghanistan. To protect their turfs and to establish supremacy they went at each other, tooth and nail, and in the process laid waste to Afghanistan.[86] Contrary to the general belief, Pakistan had no hand in this destruction. The Pakistani leadership in fact did their utmost to bring the feuding warlords onto a negotiating table, but it was to no avail. When all else failed, the Pakistanis put together a new force who were called the Taliban. This happened during the second term of the Pakistan People's Party Government, when Benazir Bhutto became the Prime Minister. General Nasirullah Babar was the Minister of interior at that time and accompanied by the American ambassador, went to Quetta to meet some 'guests' from Kandahar. Immediately after that meeting, the Taliban rose out of nowhere and reached the outskirts of Kabul. Thereafter, within a few days with the exception of one province under the control of the 'Northern Alliance,' they occupied almost the whole of Afghanistan. Taliban's hold on the country was broken when the Americans attacked them after 11 September 2001. The Taliban could not withstand the American carpet bombing and melted either into the countryside or slipped across the border into Pakistan, where many had homes and relatives.[68] Once the Americans captured Kabul, with the support of the foot soldiers from the Northern Alliance, their interest waned. President George Bush was in a hurry to attack Iraq and Afghanistan could wait. It was a pyrrhic victory as the ring leaders of al-Qaeda had slipped across the border into Pakistan, to wage war against the West, on another day.[86]

While Afghanistan had been held hostage, over the years, by al-Qaeda and other militant organizations, Pakistan too was not spared. The grip of the various militant factions tightened over the country. These militant organizations blamed Pakistan for its alliance with the US on the war against terror and wanted to punish it through the best way they knew how—terror.

After 9/11 when America attacked Afghanistan, it had the support of 92 nations in the world, including many Muslim countries like Pakistan, Saudi Arabia, United Arab Emirates and others. Al-Qaeda had now become an enemy to many Muslim governments, who it considered were American puppets and therefore fair game. Saudi Arabia topped the list despite the fact that it had been the major financier and a conduit for sending Arab fighters to Afghanistan.[86] The Taliban movement had started in 1996 with the help of the ISI, CIA and many countries of the Middle East. It was an irony that these very countries who themselves prohibited any kind of militant or religious activities in their own territories, had turned a blind eye to the activities of the Taliban in Afghanistan.[76]

The al-Qaeda had arrived in Afghanistan in 1992 to take part in the jihad against the Soviets. But by 1993-94 it had become closely aligned with the Taliban. Thus when the Taliban entered Kabul in 1996, taking advantage of the infighting between the various warlords, they in league with al-Qaeda elements occupied and razed Kabul to the ground. The resentment against the Taliban gained ground worldwide, when they instituted harsh and cruel punishments, which included cutting the hands of thieves, stoning to death of adulterers and public hangings of killers. One of the worst crimes perpetrated by the Taliban was the wanton destruction of the statues of Buddha in Bamiyan, a world heritage site.

This elicited international condemnation and protests at the mindlessness of the act. Similarly the treatment of women also attracted the wrath of the civilized world which condemned the Taliban as uncouth barbarians.[76]

In the infighting between the different militant factions, Pakistan was caught between 'a rock and a hard place'. Ironically, any faction that Pakistan favoured had turned renegade or did not come up to its expectations. It was the hope of the Pakistani military leadership and the ISI that there should be peace within the factions and that the group that would emerge as the leader, should be subservient to the directives from Pakistan. There was a time when the Pakistani leadership saw Afghanistan as a potential fifth province that could provide strategic depth in case of conflict with India. The Mujahideen were also looked upon as an asset who after their victory against the Soviets could be used for liberating Kashmir from India.[97] This was the plan of all military Governments which was also adopted later by the democratically elected governments of Nawaz Sheriff and Benazir Bhutto. It must be noted however, that while the two leaders were the prime ministers of the country, the real power and policy making, continued to be the domain of the military. The situation continues to this day.

When Benazir Bhutto was the Prime Minister, her Interior Minister was General Naseerullah Babar who was also responsible for Afghan affairs. The creation of the Taliban was engineered by him and on many occasions he referred to them as his children.[96] He toured Afghanistan but did not succeed in appeasing the forces opposed to the Taliban. Unfortunately, the political forces could not develop an independent vision for Afghanistan and always kowtowed to the military policy. Even the Pashtun nationalists the Awami National Party, whose founder Ghaffar Khan called himself an Afghan first and on his death was buried in Afghanistan, could not develop an independent stance and policy.

The Pakistani establishment continued to play musical chairs with Afghan warlords. Sometimes they picked Gulbadin Hekmatyar as the leader, another time it was Mujadadi or it was the Taliban who were the blue eyed boys. On the other side the Afghans were reaching the conclusion that it was Pakistan's constant interference in their internal affairs that was the major cause of their ills. That explains why Pakistan is seen, even today, as the enemy by both the political and religious leaders.[68] It is not a coincidence that in 1993 to 94, when the Taliban entered Afghanistan as a military force, a group called 'Nifad-e-Shariat Muhammdi' emerged in the Malakand division of the Pakistani province of North West Frontier (NWFP) who went to Afghanistan to help the Taliban during the American attack. Thereafter, while the Pakistan based extremist militant groups provided patronage to the Mujahideen, Taliban and al-Qaeda in Afghanistan, they also supported groups in Pakistan itself who promoted sectarianism and religious extremism. The result is that Pakistan today, is experiencing terrorism from both the internal and external forces to an extent that the very existence of the country is threatened.[81] In this background the policymakers in Pakistan, ostrich like, appear to be unaware of the new strategic imperatives of the US in Central and South Asia and are under the delusion, that in view of their strategic geographical location, the US cannot afford to ignore them.

Pakistan lost President Zia-ul-Haq and other key Generals in a plane crash on 17 August 1988. The American ambassador also died in the crash. The accident remains a mystery. There was no interest from the Americans for an in-depth investigation leading many to believe that it was perhaps the work of the CIA. It was rumoured that the Americans wanted General Zia out of the way to prevent him from extending the war through the victorious Mujahideen into the Soviet Republics and Kashmir. The Americans considered their mission accomplished with the retreat of the Soviets from Afghanistan and now wanted an early exit and to do that Zia-ul-Haq had to be jettisoned.[71]

After 11 September 2001 the Americans came back to Afghanistan, this time to eliminate their one time protégés the Taliban and their al-Qaeda supporters. Pakistani President General Pervez Musharraf faced a dilemma after the American asked him to choose sides, through an ultimatum, 'you are with us or against us.' He was being asked to abandon support for the Taliban or face consequences. Musharraf acquiesced and joined the war against the Taliban, opening the country's assets including the airbases to the Americans.

Pakistan faced a yet new dilemma, when the vanquished former Taliban fighters, who had taken refuge in Pakistan, went back to Afghanistan and attacked the US forces. This was the beginning of a new phase in Pak-American relations. The Americans lost confidence in the sincerity of the Pakistanis and blamed them for playing a double game. The Taliban too became hostile to Pakistan and vented their spleen by planting explosive devices in major cities creating a law and order problem.

Several attempts were also made by them to assassinate General Musharraf.[86]

The dual policy of Musharraf earned him a bad name in the country and the militant groups who had fought in Kashmir and Afghanistan now turned against the army. Today, these groups are actively spreading terror in all four provinces of the country. The militant groups in Afghanistan and Pakistan are driven by one overriding purpose which is to defeat the non-believers and establish an Islamic State with the Sharia as the guiding principles. Death has no meaning as paradise awaits them if they are killed.[80] This philosophy is also taught in the madrasas which have sprouted all over the tribal belt. The young students provide fresh blood and zest to the fighters on the battle front bombed by the militants.

Role of the Media

The Western world used media as a lethal weapon in the Afghan war. Their media policy included embellishing the exploits of the freedom fighters known as the Mujahideen against the Soviets. Besides US and the Western nations, Pakistan's media also played a part in orchestrating tributes to the 'freedom fighters'. The jihadists were presented to the public as heroes and their exploits, real or imaginary, described in glowing terms. The youth were enraptured by the propaganda and fired with the zeal of jihad, left their homes and went in droves to fight the war in Afghanistan.

This was the beginning of the Taliban movement. The army of young men from madrasas, marched into Afghanistan supported with arms and money by the Pakistani ISI. They were to be Pakistan's proxy in Afghanistan—part of an ambitious plan to perhaps one day, annex the country—to secure strategic depth in any future conflict with its arch enemy, India. The speed of their advance amazed many and surprised even the ISI. Many of the warlords surrendered without firing a shot and joined the movement. While the zeal of the young fighters played a part in their amazing victories, the money provided by al-Qaeda and the ISI, also was a factor, in softening the resistance. The rag tag Taliban army became a formidable force and by 2008 was in possession of almost 90 per cent of the country. The Taliban fighters had tasted victory and now wanted nothing less than absolute power in the country. Inspired by an extremist interpretation of the Quran, they imposed their archaic laws on a war weary population.

The al-Qaeda exploited the opportunity and joined in with men, money and arms. Soon, under its tutelage, the movement morphed into an anti-Western, terrorist organization. They discarded their hereto mentor and benefactor, Pakistan, and ceded control and direction to their new found ally and financier—Osama bin Laden—the founder of al-Qaeda. The genie was now out of the bottle and would not go back. The consequences would be disastrous for the region and the world. The International media played the role of enabler to the hilt. The BBC (British Broadcasting Corporation) radio service, broadcast reports of the heroic exploits of the Mujahideen (freedom fighters) against the Soviets. The programs were in Urdu and Pashtu for its listeners in Pakistan and Afghanistan. Unlike Pakistan, there was no print media or TV coverage in Afghanistan and 80 per cent of the population was dependent on the radio for news. The BBC became that source, augmented by the Jihadi media in the Muslim world. Dr Azaam, a founding member of the Egyptian Muslim Brotherhood, arrived in Pakistan to set up a special media cell in Peshawar. This cell consisted of likeminded Arab journalists, commentators, newspaper owners and representatives of various news agencies who carried on an effective propaganda war against the Soviets. Later on, the militant and extremist groups like the al-Qaeda, Pakistani Taliban and Kashmiri jihadists would use the media to propagate their cause and portray themselves as invincible warriors. By one estimate between 1984 and 1994, the number of newspapers and periodicals in Pakistan, supporting the jihadi cause, were in excess of 200. These were published in Urdu, Pashtu, Persian and Arabic and distributed through an efficient network to millions of readers. Even today there are dozens of magazines and newspapers in circulation, who support and propagate the extremist message.

The Internet and cell phone technology has also been harnessed. According to a research institute in Islamabad, the number of radio and television channels propagating Wahabism and Jihad, in different languages, number over 200. According to this institute, the number of Jihadi websites, exceed the number of radio and TV channels. These channels and websites are watched and visited by millions every day and they are not all Muslims. The CIA in its report of 2007 confirmed that the Jihadi newspapers, radio and TV channels and websites were conduits to gaining sympathy of the general public. In addition they were used as communication channels between the commanders of various militant groups. These have become tools in the hands of the militants and out of control of the state governments.

The Pakistani militants, from the very beginning of the conflict in Afghanistan, operated their own FM radio channels. It is estimated that in the tribal belt and in a number of districts of the KP province, there are over 30 unlicensed FM radio stations.[80] They are used for disseminating propaganda, announcements and preaching militant philosophy and sometimes for making threats. The broadcasts by Laskar-e-Islam (Khyber agency) and Maulvi Fazlullah (Swat) from mobile truck mounted stations were used to broadcast coded instructions to the commanders in the field, during skirmishes with the Pakistan military. Maulvi Fazlullah's broadcasts referred to as Mullah Radio became particularly notorious. He would broadcast religious sermons and exhort his listeners to join the jihad and at the same time hurl insults at his opponents. In 2009, the army finally moved in and destroyed these elusive truck-mounted mobile stations. Maulvi Fazlullah escaped to Afghanistan where he now lives, purportedly protected by Kabul based warlords and some members of the Karzai government.

Taliban and the Political Parties in Pakistan's Tribal Belt[80]

The nationalist parties like the ANP (Awami National Party) and the religious parties, JUI (Jamat-e-Ulema-e-Islam) and the JI (Jamat-e-Islami) have always been at loggerheads with each other, due to differences in ideologies. ANP is a liberal, secular party whereas the religious parties have supported the Taliban and their extremist, anti-West agenda. Post-9/11, ANP lined itself with forces who were anti-Taliban, as they considered the Taliban a disruptive force, which if not checked has the potential of bringing destruction to the region. In contrast, the Taliban were staunchly supported as they are today, by all religious parties in the country.

Unfortunately, during their current stewardship of the provincial government, ANP has been discredited with allegations of corruption, poor governance and American cronyism. Its leaders have been targeted by the Taliban in both suicide and ambush attacks. Peshawar, the capital of the KP province, is considered the most dangerous city in the country. ANP is not expected to win in the next general elections scheduled in March 2013. The party that is likely to win is the PTI (Pakistan Tehrik-e-Insaf) led by the former Pakistan cricket captain Imran Khan. He is an Oxford graduate, very charismatic and well known in the Western world as he was once married to Jemima Khan the British heiress but are now divorced. In his speeches he is anti-American and anti-war—a stance which is very popular with the masses. This may change if he is able to capture the popular vote and forms the next government in the KP province. Imran Khan is also popular in the Punjab, the largest province in Pakistan and home to 60 per cent of the country's population. He is expected to win a significant number of seats in the National Assembly (lower house) from here. If he does, he could very well form the government at the centre, and become the next prime minister of the country.

The Mindset of the Pakistani Taliban

It is the universal truth that while all religions of the world preach the virtue of mercy and compassion, tragically however, most major religions can also justify violence since their cannons also contain martial metaphors that can also be associated with terrorism. Whole books of the Hebrew Bible are devoted to the conquests of great kings. In Hinduism, warfare is the basis of great religious epics such as the Mahabharata. Warfare however, is not just confined to mythic legends. It has spilt over into history with conflicts, such as the Crusades, the Muslim conquests and the religious wars of the sixteenth century.

One feature of Islamic conquests which has drawn controversy is the concept of Jihad. Contrary to popular belief, Jihad is not a blank check for aggression, but instead, is bound by certain rules of waging war. According to the religious scholar Allama Javed Ghamdi: [80]

(1) Only a State can call for Jihad and not an individual.

(2) Jihad is called only if one is assured of success. A declaration of jihad which results in unnecessary killings (on both sides) is forbidden

(3) Women, children and the elderly are not to be harmed

(4) Cultivated fields are not to be destroyed or the trees cut down.

How then to explain the barbarity, the killing and the destruction carried out by the Taliban in the name of Islam and Jihad, and that too against fellow Muslims? The answer lies in the fact that the most extreme religious terrorist can sanction 'almost limitless violence against anyone.'[86] This distortion of the teachings of religions has been most brutal and fanatical where the blood of the faith community is made sacred 'by the fanatical utterances of the religiously and racially intoxicated'. In the ethos of the radical Islamic terrorism, for example, individuals believe in the martyrdom or self-sacrifice in the service of Allah, and have no moral 'red lines' in terms of number of casualties and the extent of destruction they are willing to inflict. They carry out violence because jihad must go on: 'in a jihad there are no red lines,' and the extent of damage or the number of casualties are of no primary importance. These are cults headed by charismatic leaders who dominate the followers spiritually and emotionally and are usually very dangerous.

Since 2004, the Taliban have targeted not only the Pakistani armed forces but also innocent civilians in big cities. The agenda is to create terror and fear in the general population, whose anger can then be directed towards the government, for its inability to protect them. As part of this terror strategy, they would kill their opponents in a manner that is a warning to all those that dare oppose them. In recent years, In Kurrum, Waziristan and Bajaur agencies the Taliban condemned to death approximately 55 individuals as spies of the US and Pakistan. These persons were then killed by slitting their throats. In Swat, approximately 34 persons were similarly condemned to death. Their bodies were thrown out in the open to be devoured by dogs and wild animals. Even the slitting of throats was carried out differently for different crimes. Those caught spying for the US had their throats slit at a lower part of the neck so that it was more painful and took them longer to die. Whereas those condemned as Pakistani spies had their throats slit like sacrificial goats which in comparison resulted in a quicker death. Before killing them, a video film was made in which the victims confessed their crimes. The videos were then disseminated in cities and villages' as a warning. Sometimes the unlucky victims were killed in a public show watched by crowds and their death celebrated with gun fire.

The same treatment was meted out to the Pakistani army soldiers and police personnel who were unlucky to be caught by the Taliban. Their pitiable pleas for mercy were recorded and then they were killed. In a one year period in 2008, approximately 5,000 people were killed in Pakistan by the Taliban which included Benazir Bhutto and other notables of the area. The practice of slitting throats, lashing of captives and brutal treatment of women was brought into the country by the Arab and Central Asian militants. This heinous method of killing and desecration of bodies and abuse has created an atmosphere of fear in the general population.

TALBAN'S RESTRICTIONS ON ARTS IN PAKISTAN

The identity and heritage of a society are depicted through the different faces of art prevalent in that culture. In time these arts become a part of history, which can be viewed with pride by the coming generations. The Pashtuns too are the inheritors of great historical traditions which are reflected in the poetry and literature of such giants as Rahman Baba and Khushhal Khan Khattak. Their works were emulated and expanded upon by Hamza Shinwari, Ghani Khan, Ajmal Khatak and Qalandar Momin. It was therefore a time of great shame for the Pashtuns, when the grave of Rahman Baba was bombed by the Taliban to prevent the people from laying wreaths, as they equated this practice with idolatry and grave worship. The truth is that any form of extremism impedes the progress of a society as the boundary between religion and culture is often murky and many a time a cultural tradition is foisted on its followers as sacred.

After 2002, the extremist Taliban groups expanded their hold in the entire KP province (former NWFP), and targeted any work of art which included music, theatre and movies. The extremist ideology of the Taliban was supported by a coalition of religious parties called the MMA (Mutahida Majlis-e-Amal) who won the provincial elections in 2002 and thus formed the provincial government. Amongst the various repressive edicts issued by this government was the closing of the Nishtar Hall in the capital, Peshawar. It was the venue for cultural stage shows, musical evenings and other entertainments in the Peshawar city. The Hall as such, remained closed from 2002 to 2008, during which thousands of individuals associated with the entertainment industry lost their livelihood. In fact, during the tenure of the MMA the Ministry of Culture was also disbanded.

The Taliban imposed similar restrictions when they took control of Waziristan, by banning the watching of TV, use of tape recorders, dish antennas and cassette/CD players in cars. The MMA government ironically, went a step further, by banning the use of cassette/CD players in public transport as well as prohibiting the use of photos/images of women on advertising billboards and cinema houses. The business community protested but to no avail and finally the IMF (International Monetary Fund) and the World Bank then declined to provide further funds for projects in the province.

The MMA government did not relent and continued to harass the artists. The offices and homes of the well-known Pashtu singers Khayal Muhammad and Gulzar Alam, were raided and the two sons of Gulzar Alam were arrested and kept in police lockup for two days. Others like Qamar Gulla and Shah Wali migrated abroad or moved out to other provinces in the country. The situation deteriorated further when the shops in the 'Royal Park' in Nishtarabad, a market for electronic items, were bombed by the militants.

Summing up, the war on culture and art which was started by the provincial government headed by the MMA was expanded by the Taliban. This was the beginning of extremism in the province which then enveloped most facets of life.

7

Militant Groups and Their Leaders

The Taliban and other militant groups have developed a hierarchy of command and control consisting of experienced commanders who have taken part in the jihad in Afghanistan.[80] At this time their leadership has two roles. One relates to policy and decision making, while the other handles military matters. In this chapter, attempt will be made to identify the prominent militant groups operating in the tribal belt of Pakistan, whose aim is to establish an Islamic caliphate in the region.

The tribal belt in Pakistan is a largely an autonomous zone straddling the boundary between Pakistan and Afghanistan. It also serves as a buffer zone between Afghanistan and Pakistan. For a long time, after Pakistan came into existence, in 1947, it was known as 'elaqa ghair' or alien territory.[11] It was also referred to as Yaghistan which means 'the land of the free.'[80] The territory comprises Dir, Swat, Buner, Asmar, Shabqadar Babra, Mohmand, Asmat and Chamaerkand. The inhabitants referred to as the 'Yaghis' or highland Pashtuns are a fiercely independent community who brook no interference from outsiders. According to a Colonel Brazier Creagh of the British army who visited the area in 1893-94, 'it is impossible to go inside and if you did, your bones would be left there.'[12]

When the British constituted the North West Frontier Province (NWFP) now known as Khyber Pakhtunkhwa (KP), the tribal areas of

Kurrum, Khyber, Malakand, North and South Waziristan, continued to be treated as 'Independent territories'. The British, during the colonial times, had extended civil administration to the settled areas such as Kohat, Peshawar, D.I. Khan and others but the highland areas were never occupied. Instead the Pakhtun tribal communities were paid 'an allowance' to protect the roads and ensure the security of the border with administered areas.[13] The colonial administration did not get involved in their affairs and instead appointed 'maliks' and 'sardars', who exercised temporal influence on the clans and tribes, while a network of clerics managed the religious affairs. This setup continued even after Pakistan came into existence and continues to this day.[25]

FATA (FEDERALLY ADMINISTERED TRIBAL AREAS)

One of the most significant events in the history of FATA and the lives of its people was the creation of Pakistan in 1947. After a long period of isolation and suffering during the British period, their dream of a Muslim state in which they would be free and equal citizens was being realized. The tribes welcomed the new state of Pakistan with one voice and without any hesitation, signed agreements to be a part of it as its loyal citizens.

There was hope that with the establishment of Pakistan, a new era of change and progress would begin for the tribal people. The tribes were optimistic that their own government, run by their own people, would in due course, correct and improve the old system of governance while framing a new constitution for Pakistan. Their optimism was reinforced by Mr. Jinnah, the founder of the country, who announced his decision to pull out all military forces from the tribal areas and to allow people the complete freedom of movement. The tribesmen reciprocated the trust and confidence reposed in them when thousands of them fought voluntarily for the liberation of Kashmir in Pakistan's first war with India. The successive constitutions of 1956, 1962 and 1973 of Pakistan, however, retained the colonial era administrative and legal system enacted in 1872 and embodied in the frontier crimes regulation (FCR 1901). This system is inherently oppressive, negative in purpose and authoritarian in spirit. It gave virtually unlimited judicial and administrative powers to the political agents to fine, blockade, detain and seize hostile groups and confiscate or destroy property in the tribal areas.

The members of the National Assembly (MNA), elected from FATA to the lower house, did not voice the true feelings of the people, as being themselves no more than glorified village elders (maliks), their own interests coincided with the continuation of the system. The larger, dominant state system bears the responsibility for continuing with the outdated parallel legal system for over six decades after Pakistan became independent of British rule.

Lack of effective representation and participation of the tribal population in the decision making process was always a sore point. At present, they are represented by 12 members in the National assembly (lower house) and eight in the Senate (upper house) but, these legislative bodies cannot make any laws for FATA, being the absolute domain of the President. FATA has no representation at the provincial level and no elections are held at the local level. With the devolution of powers to the provinces through the 18th Amendment of Pakistan's constitution, representation at the provincial level has now become critically important.

Neglected for decades, FATA is one of Pakistan's poorest regions, with reportedly over 60 per cent of the population living below the poverty line. Huge unemployment, alarmingly low literacy rates, poor health services and an underdeveloped infrastructure has set FATA apart from the rest of Pakistan. The dismal human indicators are a clear sign that the state has failed to perform its role in FATA.

Unlike previous times, the tribesmen after some reluctance welcomed all development initiatives of the government after independence. Society was well on its way to progress when it saw its natural course of change and development rudely interrupted with the arrival of thousands of Mujahideen to fight the Soviets in Afghanistan. The story of how the world abandoned Afghanistan after the Soviets capitulated is well known. But what is perhaps not known is that FATA too was abandoned, leaving it with a Jihadi mindset, an abundance of cheap modern weapons and easy entry and exit of foreign Mujahideen.

The weaponization of society and the presence of foreign extremist militants have dealt a serious blow to the tribal system. This in large part is responsible for the current imbroglio. Some people erroneously think that FATA, being a tribal society, is static and lacks any internal dynamic of change. An objective view of change in FATA is sufficient to convince one, that it is impacted just as much by events as the rest of the country.

The tribal society, once considered classless and egalitarian, has transformed considerably into a class-based society. Four distinct classes comprising the big maliks (village heads), the new rich, the educated and professionals and lastly the common masses can be identified in the tribal society. Their overall aspirations and social behaviour, towards change and reforms, is characterized by the class to which they belong.

Though appreciably impacted by modern changes, FATA's special status was retained under articles 246-247 of Pakistan's 1973 constitution. However, no serious effort was ever made by the government to reduce poverty and give effective political representation, basic human rights and a mechanism to redress grievances to this marginalized region of Pakistan. By failing to fulfill its obligations, the state appears to have abandoned FATA to its fate.

FATA has suffered heavily for being consigned to the backwaters, ignored and exploited for jihadi activities. The resulting militancy has considerably weakened the tribal infrastructure as well as the old system of governance which cannot be revived. A paradigm shift is required in approaching governance and socio economic issues in FATA. It will not be easy but the path to peace and a lasting solution lies in ending the isolation of FATA and integrating the region into the mainstream through a new social contract.[102]

MILITANT GROUPS IN FATA

1. The Haqqani Network[80]

The group is headed by Jaluluddin Haqqani who has been responsible for setting up madrasas and military training camps in the border areas between Pakistan and Afghanistan.[64] Their activities in the region, which began in 1978, continue till date and have the support of al-Qaeda, and other militant organizations.[64] Due to advancing age and health problems, Jalaluddin Haqqani has passed the mantle of leadership to his son Sirajuddin Haqqani (alias Khalifaji), who operates out of North Waziristan in Pakistan. He carries a five million dollar US bounty on his head. The group has links with foreign fighters, Pakistani Taliban (TTP) and Afghan Taliban. It operates on professional lines and has its own think tank and a political wing. The notable members of this group are Moulvi Gul Ramzan, resident of Miranshah, Moulvi Naeem, resident of Bannu and Moulvi Muhammad Saleem, resident of Waziristan and also includes many experienced guerilla fighters who hail from Central Asia and the Middle East.[80] The militant wing is overseen by two other sons of Jalaluddin Haqqani—Nasiruddin Haqqani and Badaruddin Haqqani who also supervise the operations in Kashmir. This group is vehemently anti-Shia and anti-Northern Alliance of Afghanistan. The fighters in this group number approximately 15,000.

2. Tehrik-i-Taliban, Pakistan[80]

This group was formed by Baitullah Mehsud, a leading militant in Waziristan, Pakistan. He formed the TTP from an alliance of about five militant groups in December 2007. He is thought to have commanded up to 5,000 fighters and to have been behind many attacks in Pakistan including the assassination of Benazir Bhutto which he has denied.[80] The group achieved international notoriety as mentors of Faisal Shahzad, the man who attempted to explode a car bomb in the New York city's Times Square in May 2010, and Humam Khalil Balawi, the Jordanian doctor, who killed seven CIA agents in a suicide mission in Afghanistan in January 2010.

According to the Pakistani security officials, Baithullah Mehsud, his wife and body guards were killed on 5 August 2009 in a US drone attack in the Zangar area of South Waziristan. He was succeeded by his fellow tribesman Hakimullah Mehsud. The areas where the group is active are North and South Waziristan, Kurrum, Karzai, Mehmand, Khyber and Bajaur tribal agencies. This is the only militant group which has representations in all provinces of Pakistan which includes Punjab, Sind, Khyber Pakhtunkhwa and Baluchistan. They recruit locals from these provinces and have their headquarters in a place called Makeen in South Waziristan. The prominent commanders of this group based in Pakistan are: [80]

1. Commander Hakimullah Mehsud. He took over as the head of the TTP on the death of Baitullah Mehsud.
2. Commander Faqir Dawar alias 'Doctor' of Miranshah.
3. Commander Haji Aftab Khan of Mir Ali.
4. Moulvi Abdullah: He is responsible for providing sanctuary to foreign fighters and looking after their needs.
5. Moulvi Noor Syed Amir, of Razmuk Sarobi, North Waziristan.

The Commanders located in other districts of the Khyber Pakhtunkhwa province are:

6. Commander Rahmanullah, incharge Khyber and Kurram agencies.
7. Commander Hazrat Ali of Khyber Agency.
8. Commander Umar Khalid of Mehmand Agency.
9. Haji Faqir Muhammad of Bajaur agency.

These commanders have also appointed deputies in their areas of control. For example, Umar Khalid of Mohmand agency, has appointed Qari Shakeel, Sangin Qandahari, Yar Syed, Ikramullah, Daray Khan, Wajhiullah, Shahzada, Bilal, Bukhari and commander Mausum as his deputies.[80]

Similarly, Maulvi Faqir Muhammad of Bajaur agency has appointed, Mulla Syed Muhammad, Maulvi Umar, Mahsud Salar, Commander Shina, Inayat ur Rehman and Commander Abdullah as deputies. Despite their differences, the Taliban commander, Tariq of Darra Adam Khel and Commander Qari Hussein of Khurram agency are considered associates of the TTP. The Taliban groups in Sind, Baluchistan and Swat have also sworn their allegiance to the TTP.

3. The Taliban of North Waziristan[80]

This group in the year 2007 and 2008 was a part of the TTP which at that time was headed by Baitullah Mehsud. They separated in 2008, but returned to the TTP fold in 2009. The amir (head of the group) is Hafiz Gul Bahadur of the Khel Wazir tribe. His deputy is Maulvi Nazeer who operates in South Waziristan. The Group has the protection of Mufti Nur, a notable person of the area. Some of the well-known commanders of this group are, Moulvi Elam Khan of the Khushhali Wazir tribe, Commander Mir Ali Saifullah of the Kabul Khel Wazir tribe, Commander Shewah, Commander Azad Khan (incharge Miran Shah), Commander Abu Shoaib. Gul Bahadur, the Amir, is also the Commander of the Dutta Khel district. In South Waziristan, Gul Bahadur's close supporter is Maulvi Nazir Haqqani of TTP which makes him the third most lethal force in the area. Moulvi Nazir is not friendly to fighters from Central Asia and in the year 2007, with the support of the Pakistan army, expelled the Uzbek Commander Tahir Yaldashov from the area. Gul Bahadur supported him in that mission. In 2008, another group headed by Moulvi Qari Zainuddin

Mehsud appeared on the scene with 500 fighters. This group was formed in opposition to Hakimullah Mehsud of the TTP by the Pakistani Intelligence who wished to see the TTP influence reduced if not totally eliminated from the area.

4. The Mehdi Millitia and Haidari Taliban[80]

Both these groups consist of militants of the Shia sect. The Commanders of this group are Hussein Ali Shah and Abid Hussein. They operate in the Kurrum agency against the TTP as well as a group called Tehrik-i-Taliban Islami. Both groups have a combined strength of 8,000 to 10,000 soldiers. They are supported by Iran and the Northern Alliance of Afghanistan. There is a sizable Shia population in the Kurram agency who support these groups. Also, a number of commanders from the Northern Alliance of Afghanistan are present here who have taken part in fights with TTP and Qari Hussein.

5. Lashkar-e-Islam[80]

This is an important militant group in the Khyber agency. It is headed by a local man of the Afridi tribe named Haji Mangal Bagh. It started off as a vigilante group, prosecuting local criminals and in the process gained acceptance in the population. Later, however, it adopted the Taliban practices whereby people were punished for not attending prayer services; not closing shops at prayer time and committing unsocial acts. It opposes 'Ansar ul Islam,' a local rival group, and it is estimated that approximately 600 people have been killed to date in skirmishes between the two groups. Lashkar-e-Islam has around 5,000 fighters of whom 1500 are considered battle hardened. The Peshawar city in Pakistan and its outlying areas are the Lashkar's strongholds.

6. Ansar ul Islam and Amar Bil-Maroof Wanhi-an-al-Munkir[80]

These two groups are prominent in the Khyber agency. The leader of the Bil-Maroof group, Haji Namdar Khan, was killed on August 13, 2009. They blamed the killing on Commander Hakimullah Mehsud of the TTP. Namdar was a supporter of the Afghan Taliban and opposed the TTP.

7. Tehrik-e-Nifad-e-Shariat Muhammadi (TNSM)—(Malakand Division)[80]

This group has prominence in the Malakand Division and the Swat valley. It is headed by Moulvi Fazlullah who was targeted by the Pakistan army during its operations in the Swat valley. Fazlullah escaped to Afghanistan where he lives under the patronage of the Karzai Government and some warlords. They make forays across the border into Pakistan to harass the Pakistani armed forces. The Pakistani Government has lodged protests with NATO and the Afghan Government on several occasions, asking them to restrain the group.

8. The Kashmiri Group[80]

Besides the groups mentioned above, there are others who are promoting Talibanization in the tribal belt of Pakistan as well as other parts of the Khyber Pakhtunkhwa province. These are: Lashkar-e-Tayaba (perpetrators of the Mumbai attack), Lashkar-e-Jahangvi, Sipah Sahaba, Harkat-ul-Mujahideen, Jaish-e-Muhammad and Harkat-al-Mujahideen-al-Islami who besides taking part in the Kashmir liberation activities, are also responsible for spreading sectarianism in Pakistan. These groups moved into the tribal belt after Pakistan imposed restrictions on their movements. The fighters are originally from the Punjab and Kashmir, and also have links with the Haqqani group and the TTP. The leader of Harkat-al-Mujahideen Islami, is Qazi Saifullah Akhtar and the head of Jaish Muhammad is Maulana Masud Azhar who operates in Punjab, Kashmir as well as in the Kurram and Orakzai agencies of the KP province. Their target is the Shia population who they harass with the support of the Haqqanis and the TTP. The Jihadis from the Punjab have also moved into Afghanistan supported by the Haqqani network. The infusion of funds from foreign sources, mainly Saudi Arabia, has served to promote fundamentalism in Pakistan. The strategy of these various militant groups is to ensure that they have a role in Afghanistan, post-US withdrawal.

Groups of Taliban Forces in FATA[80]

There was a time when the Taliban were known exclusively as an Afghan entity. But after capturing a wide swath of Afghan territory (prior 9/11), their real agenda became clear to their naive supporters, in Pakistan and

Afghanistan. They found out that 'Taliban' in fact, was a way of life built around an extremist interpretation of the Quran. The Taliban believed that anyone who differed with them was an apostate and therefore deserved to die. That was why when the majority of the Mujahideen fighters returned to Pakistan after the Soviets withdrew, they preached a version of Islam in which the followers of the Shia sect were declared as non-believers. The Shias were targeted indiscriminately and their places of worship destroyed. In reaction to the atrocities committed, two Shia militant groups emerged in the region, where previously there were none. These groups have the support of the Pakistani Intelligence who uses them against the TTP.

The fact is that religious intolerance reared its head during the eleven year rule of General Zia ul Haq, who did great disservice to Pakistan by creating these militant organizations, purportedly to fight in Afghanistan and Kashmir, but in reality, he used Islam as a tool to consolidate his own dictatorial rule. Taliban as such is very much the product of the machinations of a wily, power hungry General, who put his own interests before that of the nation. It is an irony, that the same Taliban has now chosen to bite the hand that fed it, and has turned against its mentor—the Pakistani army. By a conservative estimate, the number of commanders, fighters and workers in the various Taliban outfits operating in the seven tribal agencies of Pakistan are in excess of 60,000. This number does not include the Taliban fighters in the Pashtun belt of Baluchistan and in urban Sind. If these were included then their number on the Pakistan side of the border would total approximately 70,000. Numerically, the largest concentration of the Taliban forces is in South Waziristan where four prominent groups have the highest numbers of well-trained fighters. It is believed that there are approximately 35,000 to 50,000 fighters based in South Waziristan alone. Besides these fighters, there are over 300 suicide bombers at the beck and call of of Hakimullah Mehsud (TTP) and Sirajuddin Haqqani. A numerical breakdown of the fighters in South Waziristan is as follows:

Hakimullah Mehsud (TTP)	20,000 to 30,000 fighters
Maulvi Nazir Group	12,000 to 15,000 fighters
Tahir Uldashov (Uzbek)	3,000 to 4,000 fighters
Abdullah Mehsud	500 to 700 fighters

North Waziristan is also a stronghold of fighters, but numerically, these are less than South Waziristan. The numbers of Taliban fighters based here are:

Hafiz Gul Bahadur group	8,000 to 10,000 fighters
Hakimullah Mehsud (TTP)	5,000 to 8,000 fighters
Siraj Haqqani and associates	12,000 to 15,000 fighters

Siraj Haqqani and Hakimullah Mehsud have a close alliance with each other and also conduct joint training of their fighters. In fact these two commanders have been primarily involved, in the attacks on the US and NATO forces in Afghanistan.

The Orakzai Tribal Agency[80]

This is the region where the Shia and the Sunni militants are at war with each other. These factions have supporters in all three neighbouring countries; Iran, Pakistan and Afghanistan. That is why the largest number of killings has been recorded here. The two largest groups in this region are:

Hakimullah Mehsud group (TTP)	6,000 to 8,000 fighters
Hussein Ali Shah and Abid Hussein (Shia)	5,000 to 7,000 fighters

Kurram agency[80]

In this agency, Qari Hussein is a ruthless and a violent commander. He also controls a substantial number of suicide bombers. He is a supporter of the TTP and is closely associated with the Taliban in the Darra Adam Khel area which is headed by Commander Tariq.

While all these groups depend on each other's support, Hakimullah Mehsud of the TTP is the only Commander who operates single-handedly in the Kurrum, Orakzai and the Khyber agencies.

The Khyber agency[80]

Close to the city of Peshawar in Pakistan, is the Tarin Khyber agency, where like the Kurram agency, the militant groups number more than three. Here also, the adherents of the TTP group headed by Hakimullah Mehsud, is growing. Their anti-Pakistan Government and anti-Pakistan army activities have become progressively violent. The prominent groups in the area and their commanders are:

Rahmanullah (TTP)	1,000 to 1,200 Fighters
Mangal Bagh (Lashkar-e-Islam)	2,000 to 3,000 Fighters
Ansar ul Islam (Commander not known)	1,000 to 1,500 Fighters
Amar Bil Maroof (Commander not Known)	300 to 500 Fighters

Attacks on the NATO supply columns out of Pakistan have been carried out mainly by Hakimullah Mehsud's TTP group, supported at times by Lashkar-e-Islam.

Mohmand Agency[80]

Agitation began in this region, after the army operation in June 2007 against the residents of Lal Masjid (red mosque) located in Islamabad. Religious extremists including women who were students at the madrasa, located inside the mosque complex, had become vigilantes against prostitution and gambling. When appeals to desist and vacate the mosque failed, the Government under General Pevez Musharraf used military force, as a result of which a large number of occupants including women and the head of the madrasa were killed. The military action against the mosque resulted in nationwide protests as well as by the militant group in the area led by Commander Umar Khalid a member of the TTP. The number of fighters under him is estimated at 5000.

Bajaur Agency[80]

This is the part of South Waziristan, where the Pakistan army carried out an operation against the Taliban towards the end of 2008, in which approximately 1,500 Taliban fighters were killed. Also 950 fighters were arrested which included a large number of foreign fighters. The Pakistan army lost 74 soldiers killed in action and 270 injured. In the process, approximately 200,000 to 300,000 people were uprooted from their homes.

The composition of the Taliban and other militant forces in the Bajaur agency is as follows:

Maulana Faqir Muhammad (TTP)	4,000 to 5,000 fighters
Commander Zia ur Rahman (Lashkar Islam)	1,500 to 2,000 fighters
Zarqavi Group (Arab fighters)	700 to 1,000 fighters
Al Zawahiri Group (Arab fighters)	600 to 900 fighters

Besides the seven tribal agencies, there are the semi-tribal areas where there is a large concentration of Taliban fighters. The Swat valley was cleansed of the Taliban militants by the Pakistan army, towards the end of 2008. Before the army action there were approximately 11,000 Taliban fighters based in the Swat valley. The large number of Taliban fighters is a proof of the fact that after 2002, they have organized themselves into a lethal force, in the tribal areas of Pakistan. The Pakistani Taliban were trained by the al-Qaeda Islamic Movement of Uzbekistan, Afghan Taliban and other Jihadi movements, in modern warfare, and have becomefamiliar with latest military equipment in use by the NATO forces. They are a match for any conventional army as attested by the determined resistance they have put up against the Pakistan army over the last six years.

FOREIGN MILITANT GROUPS IN PAKISTAN'S TRIBAL BELT[80]

As mentioned in the previous pages, volunteer fighters known as the 'Mujahideen' and their mentors from the Islamic countries entered Afghanistan, to fight the Soviet army during the jihad. However, once the Soviets capitulated, these militants joined the Taliban in spreading their extremist version of Islam in Afghanistan and Pakistan.

The situation changed post 9/11 when America occupied Afghanistan which put the extremist groups in a quandary. The militants, who retreated over the border to Pakistan, could not return home as their governments had imposed a ban on all religious activities as well as frozen their bank accounts. The militants therefore had to find sanctuary in the tribal belt of Pakistan, where in fact, many settled down after marrying into the local tribes.

It may be noteworthy to mention here, that the Chinese government, at one time, had blamed a Pakistani religious party for inciting rebellion in their Muslim majority Sinkiang province. In fact, one of the foreign militant groups, which participated in the Afghan jihad, is the Chinese Uighur group which is now stranded in Pakistan and cannot return home, for fear of prosecution. The presence of the Chinese Uighurs in the country is a source of great embarrassment to the Pakistan government, which values its friendship with China, but helpless as it has little or no control over them. The other foreign militias operating in Pakistan include: al-Qaeda, Islamic Movement of Uzbekistan and three or more militant groups out of Turkmenistan. These organizations operate alongside the Tehrik-e-Taliban Pakistan (TTP) and Afghan Taliban but ensure their separate identity by deploying platoons of own ethnic makeup. These foreign fighters use Waziristan, Kurrum and Bajaur agencies in Pakistan as their bases. They have been targeted by the US and NATO forces with drones, resulting in the death of many fighters. The drone operations continue till date, purportedly with the tacit support of Pakistani authorities. [80]

By one conservative estimate, approximately 1,500 to 2,500 militants belonging to the al-Qaeda factions have taken part in operations within Pakistan. In the year 2007-08, the al-Qaeda militants attacked the Pakistani security posts in the Bajaur agency. They also attacked the government forces in Waziristan as well as the Shia militant groups in the Kurrum agency. A large number of these foreign militants have been arrested in the Pakistani cities of Peshawar, Mianwali, Faisalabad, Rahim Yar Khan, Multan, Jacobabad, Quetta and Karachi. The militants arrested to date number over 1000. Those arrested have invariably been handed over to the US.

The Arab fighters belonging to the al-Zarqavi and al-Zawahiri factions, number between 1,500 and 3,000. These militants make incursions into Afghanistan to hit the US and the NATO troops and then return to their base camp in Bajaur. The Zarqavi faction comprise of fighters from Jordan, Iraq and Syria. Their leader is Doctor Muhammad Ismail, who belongs to Jalalabad, the capital of the Nangarhar province in Afghanistan. It is not known whether the title 'Doctor' is an alias or he is a medical graduate. The Al Zawahiri group consists of fighters from Egypt, Iraq and Saudi Arabia. Ayman Al Zawahiri, the al-Qaeda leader, has been in regular contact with this group and there are reports that he spent some time in Bajaur and Chitral. The commander of this group is also named Ismail and he belongs to the Kunar province in Afghanistan. The fighters number approximately 1000. They essentially plan the operations conducted in Pakistan and Afghanistan. Majority of the members have been associated with Osama bin laden and Ayman al Zwahiri from the beginning of the Afghan Jihad. This group also uses Bajaur as their base from which they carry out raids into Afghanistan's Kunar and Nuristan provinces and other areas of eastern Afghanistan. This group has also been targeted by the US drones beginning 2006 to date. Within al-Qaeda, there are two schools of thought. One supports the terrorist activities within Pakistan, while the other sees them as counter productive and in fact counsels the militant groups such as the Tehrik-e-Taliban Pakistan (TTP) and others to desist and instead concentrate on hitting only the US and NATO forces across the border.

According to the US sources there are as many as 5,000 to 11,000 foreign fighters in Pakistan, who are associated with al-Qaeda. These militants are based in Waziristan, Kurrum and Bajaur agencies as well as in some parts of Baluchistan and in Southern Punjab. These militants include fighters from North and South Waziristan as well as from Uzbekistan, Tajikistan and Chechnya and the Uighurs from China. The leader of the Uzbek group, Qari Tahir Yaldeshov, in fact lived in the Mehsud (TTP) strongholds of Makeen and Ladha from 2006 to 2008 and took part in terrorist activity alongside them. In 2007, some Taliban factions expressed resentment against these foreign fighters and soon fighting broke out between them and the Taliban factions headed by Hafiz Gul Bahadur and Maulvi Nazir. The foreign militants including Tahir Yaldashov were forced to leave the area. During the fighting, a large number of foreign militants were killed and their homes burnt down. On the other hand, there are many Uzbek and Tajik fighters who have eschewed fighting after marrying local women and have settled down to a peaceful way of life.

Besides al-Qaeda and the Islamic Movement of Uzbekistan (IMU), the Uighur militants from China are the third notable foreign group, operating in the country. The acronym for their movement is Islamic Movement of Freedom (IMF). By a conservative estimate, in the year 2007-08, there were 50 to 300 Chinese Uighur fighters based in Waziristan and fought alongside the TTP. The leader of the group is a man called Obaidullah who hails from Sing kiang.

SOURCES OF TALIBAN FUNDING

Adequate finance is essential to the survival and expansion of any revolutionary movement. And, if this becomes a rebellion or an armed conflict, then acquisition of arms becomes a top priority. The Taliban movement in Pakistan and Afghanistan has now existed for over a decade but the momentum, instead of diminishing, has continued to grow over the years and the Pakistan army despite its proclaimed professionalism has failed to stem the tide.[80]

One explanation, frequently heard, is that these Pashtun militants, on both sides of the divide, are a war like people who are adept in guerrilla warfare. Another reason given is that these fighters are equipped with modern arms which make them hard to beat. The question therefore arises as to how these militants are acquiring the arms, and what is the source of their funding? For example, there are some militant groups who are flush with money and regularly pay a salary to their fighters, on the first Friday of each month, thus providing employment to tens of thousands in the region. The Taliban have been fighting the Government forces and other opponents for years and yet seem to be more than adequately supplied with money and arms. It is believed, that in addition to the small arms, these militants also have in their possession rocket launchers, tanks, armoured cars and even chemical weapons. Also, in a report issued by the 'Home Ministry' of the Khyber Pakhtunkhwa, dated 5 April 2009, it was stated that the arms and the communication equipment in use by the militants is far superior to that of the government forces. The report attributes the poor performance of the security forces to their inferior equipment. That could explain, why these militants have become bolder over time.[80]

In the beginning it was generally believed that the arms to the Pakistani Taliban (TTP) had come from al-Qaeda and the Afghan Taliban. Also, In the years prior to 9/11, when The Taliban came to power in Afghanistan, the Pakistan government along with Saudi Arabia had recognized the Taliban regime (the third country was the United Arab Emirates) and had provided it, with substantial quantity of arms and ammunition for their fight against the Northern Alliance. The Taliban also captured vast stores of military equipment when they succeeded in defeating the Afghan warlords in the provinces. After their defeat by the Americans, post 9/11, they succeeded in stashing some of these arms in their ethnic strongholds, in Afghanistan and Pakistan, which are now being utilized.[70]

From 2002 to 2004, when the Taliban were ousted from Afghanistan by the Americans, they unobtrusively began setting up bases in Waziristan and the neighbouring areas, in the hope of resuming their operations one day. They developed contacts with the religious parties in Pakistan, to harness their support, in gaining sympathy of the population. In 2004, the Taliban decided to turn their guns on Pakistan—their former mentors—who they believed had now turned into American puppets. They attacked police and military posts and created terror in cities by planting explosive devices. To finance their activities they robbed banks and kidnapped people for ransom. A list of well to do Pashtuns living in Karachi, the commercial hub of the country, was prepared so that they could be tapped from time to time, for funds. The Taliban also collected in the name of charity from individuals belonging to the tribal belt and those who did business in the Taliban controlled areas, were required to pay a protection fee. To build up their arsenal of arms, the Taliban raided the police checkposts and arms storage depots. They also set up small arms factories in partnership with gun smiths in Darra Adam Khel, who were known for their expertise in making copies of weapons including Kalashnikovs and others. In addition, these militant groups solicited financial support from notable International Jihadi outfits and Islamic NGOs through the al-Qaeda network.

Opium as Source of Funding

Afghanistan today is the largest supplier of opium in the world. It is grown right under the noses of over 140,000 US and NATO troops based there. The Afghan economy relies on two revenue streams.[98] One flows from Western aid, in the hopes that the country will renounce the Taliban. The other flows from opium trafficking supported by the Taliban, which use the proceeds to fund attacks on Western troops. Only recently has the Afghan government seemed to take stock of the obvious: for the outside world's largesse to continue, the national economy's addiction to opium must end. The poppy fields must be destroyed. But just as this devoutly Muslim nation did not become the world's leading opium supplier overnight, uprooting Afghanistan's poppy mind set promises to be a complicated endeavour.

For centuries, opium wafted over Afghanistan before engulfing it altogether. Though Alexander the Great could not totally conquer this rugged northeastern flank of the Persian Empire in the fourth century BC, he is credited with leaving behind the drug that ultimately would.[25] Actual cultivation of poppy shows up in Afghanistan's recorded history about 300 years ago. Only in the middle of the twentieth century did Afghanistan become an opium exporter.[31] At the request of the United Nations, which Afghanistan joined in 1946, King Muhammad Zahir Shah temporarily halted cultivation. The subsistence poppy farmers of Badakhshan and Nangarhar persuaded him to reverse his decision.

So it was, until the Soviet invasion of December 1979 upended Afghanistan's landscape. The new occupiers closed off the markets for several of the country's fruits and shut off the cotton gins so as to benefit Uzbekistan's exports. The ensuing decade-long war between the Soviets and the US-backed Mujahideen claimed farm-to-market roads, irrigation canals, silos, food processing factories among its victims. Afghanistan's agriculture was ruined.[68] Between the Soviet withdrawal in 1989 and the Taliban's emergence in 1994, the country descended into chaos as the warlords competed for power. India and Pakistan had succeeded in cracking down on their own opium production—and drug smugglers began to eye new pockets of instability where illegal trafficking could thrive. Consequently, though Pakistan eradicated its opium production, the problem only got pushed across the border into Afghanistan.

These are among reasons Afghanistan's share of worldwide opium production skyrocketed from 19 per cent in 1986 to 90 per cent two decades later.[71] The greatest factor, however, was the Taliban. When it first came to power in 1996, the new Islamist government garnered support from tribal leaders by agreeing not to crackdown on poppy cultivation. The supreme leader Mullah Omar received regular funding from trafficking groups which he allowed to operate freely. At the same time, the new Afghan government levied 10 per cent tax on all agricultural profits. By 1999 the opium production spiked to more than 5000 tons prompting pressure from UNODC (United Nations Office for Drug Control) for a crackdown. In July 2000 Mullah Omar issued a fatwa, or religious decree, declaring opium production a violation of Islam. The Taliban enforced the ban with brutal efficiency by threatening to set the farmers houses on fire. The result was a massive 91 per cent reduction in poppy growing in one year.[74]

After the US-led invasion of Afghanistan and the fall of the Taliban in 2001, the regional warlords once again cranked up opium production. Now, no longer in power, the Taliban saw opium as a way to fund their insurgency. They saw the opportunity to generate a tremendous amount of income without sacrificing the subsistence of the people.[98] Poppy is a winter crop, so after harvest in late spring, a farmer can plant cotton, corn or beans in the same soil. During years when demand is high, a farmer might make as much as six times more from opium than any other crop. When the price is low, the farmer can wrap his durable product in plastic and store it until the market is more lucrative.[76] It is now believed by some, that the Taliban had a large stock of opium when they enforced the ban in 2000 and were deliberately curtailing supplies to drive up the prices.

As the Taliban have gained control of southern Afghanistan over the past several years, growing poppies has only become easier. Drug traffickers advance farmers money for the harvest and later arrive to pick up the product. The drug mafia sees to it that the routes to heroin processing labs in the borderlands and then out of Afghanistan are well cleared and appropriate individuals bought off. This explains how so many low-paid officials were able to buy fancy houses in Dubai and the US.

NATO estimates that currently, insurgents, including the Taliban, get half of their financing from drugs, nearly half a billion dollars. The Afghanistan's opium economy is expected to grow beyond 4 billion dollars a year—a significant potential to feed the insurgency, by Taliban and others.[98]

8

THE ISSUES IN FATA—A HISTORICAL PERSPECTIVE

Historically, the border between Eastern Afghanistan and the Pakistan's tribal belt (FATA) has been practically non-existent. The Pashtuns who live on both sides of the divide are united by a common language and traditions.[13] The Afghans never really accepted the Durand line as the boundary, which the British drew between Afghanistan and British India in 1893. That was the stance of communist rulers during the Soviet occupation as well as the Pakistan supported Taliban/Mujahideen, who ruled in Kabul during the period 1990 to 2000, and remains unchanged now under the Karzai Government.[17]

Some factions of the Taliban play on the nationalist sentiments and justify their claim on Pakistan territory as a Pashtun struggle against Pakistan, who is dubbed as the occupier. This parochial stance received further impetus when the Americans, after their victory over the Taliban in 2001, excluded the Pashtuns, (who constitute over 45 per cent of the population) from the Afghan national Government in favour of the Persian speaking Northern Alliance minority.[87] In retaliation, the Taliban, who are predominantly Pashtuns, took up arms against the Americans—the infidel occupiers—and a violent interpretation of the religion became the tool to exhort the masses to rise in a jihad against the foreign occupation. In neighbouring Pakistan the Taliban unleashed terror on the masses by attacking army and police installations justifying their acts by branding the government and officials as apostates. Pakistan has paid a high price in this war against extremism and terror. To date over 30,000 civilians and 5000 army personnel have been killed in fighting this war.

Actually, the foundation of extremism and religious fundamentalism was laid, the day the Americans exited the region soon after the Soviets capitulated in 1986. The resulting power vacuum led to a disastrous civil war. The warlords in their quest for power razed Kabul to the ground. The hatred they garnered from the misery inflicted on the population, opened the way for the Taliban, who promised restoration of law and order as well as the introduction of an efficient justice based on Quran and Sunnah. Despite misgivings from many quarters, they actually delivered on these promises and thus gained popularity with the masses. The justice they meted out was medieval but it worked. Crime disappeared from the street and a sense of optimism prevailed. Those were heady days for the Taliban who were welcomed as saviours wherever they went. Even veteran warlords surrendered to them without firing a shot.

The goodwill however, did not last very long. The interesting ingredients of the Taliban beliefs were, first, that politics divides society and therefore democracy is irrelevant to Afghan society. Secondly, the primary task of governance is to ensure security for the people. Thirdly social and political order should be rooted in Islam. The majority of the Taliban cadres were Pashtuns. Apart from them, recruits came in from Islamic organizations from number of Muslim countries stretching from Libya and Egypt in the North to Sudan and the Gulf in the South. The Taliban were equipped by the US and the ISI with sophisticated artillery and anti-aircraft weapons, apart from the armor. They believed that the state structures and political management of civil societies should be organized on the basis of orthodox tenets of Islam, the Hadith and the Sharia.[68] They believed that both civil and criminal laws should be rooted in Sunni Islamic theology. In the initial years, the Taliban showed great capacity for discipline, austerity, military decisiveness and at times a high level of violence. By the end of 1998, the Taliban had established control over 29 provinces of Afghanistan leaving just the Panjsher valley and Mazar-e-Sharif under the control of the rival Northern Alliance leaders. Taliban imposed a strict and orthodox Islamic regime in all areas under their control. The Sharia became the supreme law in Afghanistan. Orthodox Islamic personal and social behaviour became mandatory. Males were required to grow beards, women were to be under strict purdah (seclusion). Women's education and employment was banned. Criminal justice was patterned on the Sharia law and implemented by the clergy and the Taliban with ferocious promptness. It must, however, be said to the credit of the Taliban, that there was a sharp decline in crime and corruption. The law and order situation improved though on the basis of draconian measures.[68]

As a result of the civil war and hardships imposed by the Taliban, almost 3 million Afghans poured across the border into Pakistan. The refugee camps, which Pakistan set up soon filled to the brim. The refugees were not restricted and were free to move around. The presence of the refugees caused considerable resentment in the local population who blamed them for the rise in crimes in the cities and demands were made to stop the inflow. The unemployed youth in the camps also became easy targets for recruitment by militants and drug mafias. The mullahs and the religious political parties in Pakistan saw the refugees as potential voters and stirred the pot, in their own self-interest, with anti- American and anti-government harangues. This only served to alienate the youth who succumbed to the pull of the extremist ranks which included the Taliban and other militias, stoking new insurgencies in Afghanistan and Pakistan.

It is a fact, that the common cause of insurgencies anywhere in the world is deprivation and poverty. The Pakistan's tribal belt (FATA), for the same reason, has become a haven for the extremist militant groups like al- Qaeda, Taliban and the Kashmiri groups who set up recruiting and training centres during the Afghan jihad. The following statistics provide a picture of the prevailing conditions in the area.[80]

FATA at a Glance

Area: 27,220 square kilometers
Population: 3.176 million
Density: 117 persons per square kilometer
Annual Growth Rate: 2.19%
Literacy: both sexes 17.2%
Male 29.5%
Female 3.0%
Administrative set-up: Seven agencies and six Frontier Regions Important
Mountain Passes: Khyber, Nawa, Peiwar Kotal, Tochi, Gomal

Important Rivers: Bara, Kurram, Gomal, Tochi, Taki Zam
Mountain Ranges: Off Shoots of Hindu Kush, Sulaiman and Koh Sufaid
Highest Peak: 15,620 ft Sikka Ram in Kurram agency.

LITERACY

According to a World Bank survey, the FATA region is the most illiterate in Pakistan. The overall literacy rate is about 17.2 per cent which ranges between 29.5 per cent for males and 3 per cent for females. The FATA region came out poorly even in comparison with the rest of the Khyber Pakhtunkhwa Province (former NWFP).[80]

EDUCATIONAL INSTITUTES IN FATA VERSUS THOSE IN THE ENTIRE PROVINCE OF KHYBER PUKHTUNKHWA

Primary Schools in K.P.:	22,668	Primary Schools in FATA:	3779
Number of Colleges in K.P.:	128	Colleges in FATA:	18
Number of Universities in K.P.:	15	Universities in FATA:	Nil

There were only three colleges for women in FATA which were closed down after Taliban took control. On the positive side, Pakistan established educational institutions for the 3 million Afghan refugees who arrived in Pakistan during the Afghan Jihad. These institutions were set up with the aid provided by the US, Saudi Arabia and other friendly nations.

Primary Schools for refugees set up in 1983-84:	495
Of these, the schools for girls numbered:	110

In addition special seats were reserved for the Afghan refugee students in higher educational institutions throughout the country.

Number of seats reserved in Medical Colleges:	56
Seats reserved in Engineering Colleges:	38
Seats reserved in the Islamic University, Islamabad:	78
Seats reserved in Colleges for General Sciences and Art:	150

Between 1984 and 1990, the US contributed 6.4 million dollars to Afghan madrasas (religious schools) and technical training schools. Ironically, the same madrasas have today become nurseries for extremist Taliban militants who are targeting US forces in Afghanistan.

Opportunities for Earning a Livelihood in FATA[80]

The share in Government jobs in FATA is approximately 2.3 per cent. Over 60 to 70 per cent in this region live below the poverty line. As a result, roughly 40 per cent of the population is forced to seek employment in other provinces or in the Middle East. Unemployment in the region is estimated by the Government sources at 60 to 65 per cent. The cultivable land is 0.2 per cent, forests account for 0.3 per cent of the land mass and Industry constitutes 0.1 per cent of the region's economy. According to the World Bank, 40 per cent of the tribes in the area have no electricity, 48 per cent have no clean water and 45 per cent have no access to health care.

Ostensibly, followers of the firebrand cleric Mullah Fazlullah rose up to implement the Sharia in Swat. But, their main target was the land owning local elites—the Khans—many of whom were killed and their property destroyed. Subsequently, scores of NGOs and think tanks initiated surveys and distributed surveys to help seek an answer to the question whether poverty has anything to do with militancy and Pakistan's tribal belt (FATA). Political observers were keen to establish a link between the killing spree and poverty in the troubled swaths of Swat and FATA. A vocal section of analysts abandoned the argument that declared militancy a byproduct of jihadi ideology and nothing else.

Most importantly, these findings do not hold any agency responsible for the ongoing violence in the region. Nor does it address the symbiotic relationship that exists between religious extremism and factors such as organized crime, a pervading sense of deprivation amongst the youth, the role of institutions in promoting radicalism and the state's willingness to outsource its monopoly on violence and so on.

More misleading of all has been the dominant official narrative, which holds militancy as an imported phenomenon with its roots across the border in Afghanistan. Of late, however, political observers have linked radical extremism to more pragmatic concepts such as poverty. In a recently concluded international conference in Islamabad 'Securing a Frontline State,' some researchers were of the opinion that poverty in the restive tribal belt provides a reason for the militancy to grow. "The most food insecure districts are the worst militancy hit areas," according to Dr. Abid Suleri, an expert on sustainable development.[102]

Other scholars are cautious about accepting this argument but do not reject it outright. "Yes, poverty has an important role to play, but it is not the engine of militancy; it is the fodder," says Abdullah Jan, a PhD fellow in the US. Amidst both these arguments lies the fact that radical ideologues at the top may not necessarily be representing the poor, but thousands of youth constituting the rank and file of militant groups usually come from a poor background. The given context makes it vital for researchers to avoid a top to bottom approach in studying the increasingly political role of the commanders and instead, focus more on youngsters, who are used as tools to keep militancy thriving in the troubled parts of the country.

Militancy draws its foot soldiers mainly from the marginalized rural areas, where growing disparity has virtually paralyzed the lower strata of society. Those who fail to identify with their local social system, lose their sense of ownership as well. When militancy was at its peak in Swat, a teacher serving in a roadside school talked of his ex-students not being able to continue their education because of poverty, and then upon joining Fazlullah, looking at teachers as their arch enemies. Later on the Swat Taliban—with their poor rural background—blew up over 700 schools partly because these schools did not help them change their social status in any way.

Can one separate the issue of human development from growing insecurity? Not anymore. Both are interlinked where one is causing the other. This issue has serious dimensions in FATA where no mechanism is in place even to measure the indicators of development. Violence has become perennial, causing widespread displacements. This deplorable situation has left few options to the tribal youth other than choose between starvation and a life in the IDP camps and militancy.

Awareness about the role of various Pakistani state agencies in aiding and abetting a violent culture is another important issue crucial to the understanding of religious militancy. Such agencies have always set the mood for disruptive tendencies to grow. But this supportive role is usually ignored, which has helped extremist elements give a radical underpinning to the public discourse.

The role of state agencies is combined with that of non-state religious elements, including certain madrasas and religious groups, producing a mechanism so well knit that nonsensical ideas often end up as the dominant discourse. As a result, people start seeing a US hand behind the gas shortages, rising petrol prices and the general inflation in the country. This trend has resulted in an atmosphere in which emotions have superseded reason. This reactionary culture provides a fertile ground for radicalism to grow and prosper. All the contributing factors, ideology at least, has less to do with militancy in the FATA and the Khyber Pukhtunkhwa province. Interestingly this factor has long been associated with extremism. Had the perception been correct, young militants hailing from the Mehsud, Waziri and Afridi tribes in South Waziristan, North Waziristan and the Khyber Agency would not have rallied around their respective tribal commanders. Interaction with the militants can help understand this observation where one can find their limited worldview coloured by tribal factors and revenge motives.

To defeat militancy, it has become indispensible to understand the culture honing extremism. The latter exists because Pakistani institutions are supportive of it, public discourse does not discourage it, and a sense of deprivation fuels it and also the country's intellectuals misinterpret it and the media romanticizes it. More so the country's researchers study militancy in a top-to-bottom context. They are more interested in understanding what militant commanders are doing and what is on their minds. It is least important to them to find out how young foot soldiers are influencing their leadership and how a reactionary culture rooted in their sense of deprivation is influencing them at the bottom.

Strident militancy has already turned the social and administrative system upside down in FATA. The presence of a large constituency of disoriented youth makes future prospects grim. Now is the time to reconsider official priorities. No reform agenda can serve its purpose in FATA, unless Pakistani policy makers stop thinking of tribesmen in their own colonial way. Incorporating practical measures aimed at reforming tribal youth has become inevitable for defeating the culture of militancy. Otherwise militancy, while it might change form, will stay institutionalized in Pakistan, for a long time to come.

9

Is Taliban Losing its Clout?

For many military commanders of the Tehrik-e-Taliban (TTP) who operate from FATA, reconciliation with the Pakistan government appears to have become a priority. Some believe these overtures of peace as a ruse to extract concessions from the government. However, there is a feeling that one is witnessing the beginning of the end of TTP, which is losing its clout by turning religious militancy into gangsterism.

Harassed by Pakistan's military operations and US drone strikes, the once-formidable TTP has splintered into more than 100 smaller factions, weakened and running short of cash, according to security officials, analysts and tribesmen from the insurgent heartland.[92] The group, allied with al-Qaeda and based in the northwest close to the Afghan border, has been behind much of the violence tearing apart Pakistan over the last four and a half years. Known as the Tehrik-e-Taliban, or TTP, the Taliban want to oust the US-backed government and install a hardline Islamist regime. They also have international ambitions and trained the Pakistani-American who tried to detonate a car bomb in New York City's Times Square in 2010.

'Today, the command structure of the TTP is splintered, weak and divided and they are running out of money,' said Mansur Mehsud, a senior researcher at the FATA Research Center.[80] 'In the bigger picture, this helps the army and the government because the Taliban are now divided.'

The first signs of cracks within the Pakistani Taliban appeared after its leader, Baitullah Mehsud, was killed in a drone strike in August 2009. Since then, the group has steadily deteriorated. Set up in 2007, the Pakistani Taliban is an umbrella organization created to represent roughly 40 insurgent groups in the tribal belt plus al-Qaida-linked groups headquartered in Pakistan's eastern Punjab province. 'In the different areas, leaders are making their own peace talks with the government, Mehsud added. 'It could help the Pakistani government and military to separate more leaders from the TTP and more foot soldiers from their commanders.'

The two biggest factors hammering away at the Taliban's unity are US drone strikes and Pakistani army operations in the tribal region. Turf wars have flared as militants fleeing the Pakistani military operations have moved into territory controlled by other militants, sometimes sparking clashes between groups. And as leaders have been killed either by drones or the Pakistani army, lieutenants have fought among themselves over who will replace them. 'The disintegration has accelerated with the Pakistan military operation in South Waziristan and the drone attacks by the United States in North Waziristan,' Mahsud said, referring to the two tribal agencies that are the heartland of the Pakistani Taliban. Another factor is the divide-and-conquer strategy Pakistan's military has long employed in its dealings with militants. Commanders have broken away from the TTP and set up their own factions, weakening the organization. Battles have broken out among the breakaway factions, and in one particularly remote tribal region the TTP was thrown out. These growing signs of fissures among the disparate groups that make up the Pakistani Taliban indicate that the military's strategy could be paying off.

That would explain the mixed signals coming out of the tribal belt, where some militants are mulling the idea of peace talks with the government, others are offering to stop fighting and still others are disavowing both peace and a ceasefire. It might also explain a steady decline in suicide attacks in Pakistan, according to the privately run Pak Institute for Peace Studies.

The US is eager to see some benefits in neighbouring Afghanistan, where its troops have come under attack from militants based across the border in Pakistan. NATO forces in Afghanistan are trying to break the back of the Afghan insurgency before the end of the US-led coalition's combat mission in 2014.

There is no evidence so far that fissures within the militant structure in Pakistan are helping NATO and US forces. The deadly Haqqani network, which has bases both in Pakistan and Afghanistan and is affiliated with al-Qaeda, is one of the most lethal threats to coalition troops. It has long found safe haven in Pakistan's tribal belt and has used the Pakistani Taliban as a source of recruits. Senior US officials say the Haqqanis also receive support from Pakistan's army and intelligence agency, a charge Islamabad denies.

Analysts predict that over time, however, the internecine feuding in the Pakistani Taliban will take a toll on militants fighting in Afghanistan, making it increasingly difficult for them to find recruits and restricting territory available to them. Pakistan's military has rebuffed appeals from Washington to take on all of the insurgent groups in the tribal region, saying it has neither the men nor the weapons to do so. Instead, Islamabad has pushed its divide-and-conquer approach, which is gaining some traction in the United States.

Cooperation between the US and Pakistan suffered a serious setback when NATO aircraft killed 24 Pakistani soldiers at two border posts. The 26 November 2011 incident seems certain to blunt any prospect of Pakistan taking direct steps to curb the Haqqani network. In the wake of the attack, intelligence sharing has stopped, military-to-military contact has been suspended, routes supplying non-lethal goods to NATO in Afghanistan have been shut, and Pakistan has withdrawn its offer to bring Taliban and representatives of the Haqqani network to the negotiating table. Pakistan also boycotted the conference in Bonn, Germany, in December 2011, to find ways to stabilize Afghanistan.

There is no independent figure on how many Taliban fighters operate in the tribal regions, but it is estimated to be in the vicinity of 70,000 thousand.[80] There are upward of 130 groups in the area, some of them small, violent offshoots of larger groups.

They have varying loyalties to a handful of key commanders like Hakimullah Mehsud, the current leader of the Pakistani Taliban. Popular support dwindled for Hakimullah after his group was driven out of South Waziristan by the military and relocated to North Waziristan, according to tribesmen in the area.

The Pakistani army has brokered agreements with some Taliban factions. But there are no peace talks underway with Hakimullah Mehsud, who has declared war on the state of Pakistan, the official said. A brash and heavy-handed insurgent, Mehsud has killed former allies, defied orders from the Haqqani network's chief and developed close links with criminal gangs who kidnap, extort and exploit the local population. He also has made enemies of former lieutenants in other parts of the tribal region, like neighbouring Kurram Agency, where a deputy, Fazl Saeed Haqqani, split with Mehsud three months ago and formed his own Islami-Tehrik-e-Taliban group. In yet another tribal region of Orakzai, where Mehsud once held sway, members of feuding groups are now killing one another.

The rot began in South Waziristan, the nerve centre of the TTP, where the Pakistan government launched a military operation in the Taliban controlled Mehsud area in March 2009. Unlike the past, this time the security establishment did not sign any peace deals with the militants. The TTP strength was whittled away as the operation continued.

Half a million Mehsuds were forced out of the area and most saw their homes demolished. The treatment was shocking but effective nonetheless. It was aimed at sending a message to all players in the tribal war theatre that the government meant business this time, at least in dealing with the TTP.

Surrounded by the rival Ahmedzai Wazir tribe, the TTP's powerbase has become its Achilles heel. Its central leadership was aware of their less than strategic location. Therefore, it always tried to avoid internal dissent and cobbled together political alliances to overcome external threats.

This blend of power and diplomacy helped the TTP to secure its base in South Waziristan. As long as its late chief Baitullah Mehsud was alive, the policy was instrumental in helping the TTP outsource militancy as a profitable enterprise to adjoining districts and down country.

In the post Baitullah scenario, however, the TTP leadership failed to evaluate its strengths and weaknesses. A firebrand, Hakimullah, the successor to Baitullah, avoided a direct struggle with his distant Waziri cousins but did not extend any friendly gesture to them either. Consequently, in a tribal agency, where militancy is organized mainly on the basis of tribal affinities, a lukewarm TTP approach towards local politics has had a negative impact on the Mehsud clan as a whole. The outlawed TTP is considered a Mehsud enterprise as its leaders and foot soldiers come mainly from that tribe. Thousands of hapless Mehsuds are today living miserably in camps with no care from the government and complain that the government treats them all like militants.

The plight of the TTP foot soldiers is not different from that of their displaced fellow tribesmen. In tribal tradition, extending shelter to another tribe requires the seeker to follow the rules and customs set by the benefactor. If a tribe is ousted from its territory, it loses its freedom too.

Following the Pakistan military operation, the homeless Mehsud militants took refuge with pro-government commanders Maulvi Nazir in South Waziristan and Gul Bahadur in North Waziristan. But, availing this facility has made them all spineless. They are bound to do the hosts bidding. Otherwise, they would be expelled. This factor has cut down the TTP strength by rendering ineffective a sizeable portion of Mehsud foot soldiers.

After the release of a video showing TTP chief Hakimullah Mehsud along with a Jordanian bomber responsible for the death of eight Americans at a military base in eastern Afghanistan, the TTP is now wanted by the US more than ever. Ever since then the media savvy militant has been living underground. Already battered and bruised, the TTP leadership is left with no space to operate from South Waziristan due to incessant drone attacks during the last two years. In fact Mehsuds are for TTP as Arabs for al-Qaeda. The organization lost its fangs after its Mehsud workforce was neutralized. At the same time, it has reasonable decentralized tribal chapters of the TTP operating outside Waziristan. The same ideological strength, which made the TTP the only tribal ventures representing militants of all hues, became its major weakness. It reveals that tribal militants are driven more by monetary benefits and less by ideology.

Fazal Saeed Haqqani, ex-TTP commander for lower Kurrum, was the first to raise the flag of rebellion by forcing Mehsud militants out of his area. He set up his own Tehrik-e-Taliban Islamic (TTI) to escape the ongoing military operation in Kurrum Agency. The tone and tenor of Moulvi Faqir Muhammad, the deputy TTP Amir (commander) from Bajaur, has changed after the government announced its willingness to hold a dialogue with the militants. This did not sit well with the TTP who are likely to replace him with Moulvi Fazlullah of Swat, presently residing in Afghanistan. Similarly, Omar Khalid, the TTP chief for Mohmand agency, announced in an interview with BBC that they are free to negotiate a ceasefire on their own with the government.

The present fissure in TTP ranks can be attributed to four factors.

First, the non-Mehsud franchises of the TTP have realized that affiliation with the officially despised TTP central command will make them hard to survive the present generation of military operations. Secondly, reconciliation is important to retain or maintain control over lucrative trade and smuggling routes. Thirdly, winter in the cooler mountain terrains restricts the militants' movements. Last but not the least, reconciliation with the Pakistani government is indispensable for the already demoralized militant groups. They see in the peace overtures a chance to reinvigorate themselves. This urgency has compelled a few militant commanders to announce unconditional ceasefire.

Under the circumstances, if a TTP defeat in South Waziristan has brought some respite for the security forces, breakaway tendencies in the organization carry ominous prospects of gangsterism. Militant groups have already unleashed a reign of terror by supervising criminal elements, patronizing kidnapping networks, colleting toll tax and controlling trade and smuggling routes.

Can the Taliban Revive again?

The Afghan and Pakistan Taliban have announced a joint focus on fighting the US/ISAF troops in Afghanistan. What this means is that TTP will likely scale back its attacks inside Pakistan. From a myopic point of view, this will be judged as a good thing for Pakistan, in the short term. But is the formation of Shura-i-Murakbah, a five member council representing the who's who of militancy, the Waliur Rehman, Hakeemullah Mehsud, Gul Bahadur, Mullah Nazir and the Haqqani groups, in any way a welcome development for Pakistan?

First the caveats. There is still some uncertainty about the extent to which the agreement between the Afghan Taliban and parts of the TTP can be enforced. The splintering of the TTP in Pakistan has lead to many offshoots with agendas of their own. Even the 'big five' represented in the Shura-i- Murakbah, it is not clear to what extent they will reorient towards Afghanistan to the exclusion of activities inside Pakistan. Having said that, the danger to Pakistan is a broader one. With sections of the Pakistani Taliban announcing their intentions to focus on Afghanistan, has Pakistan slipped closer to being labeled as a 'sponsor of terrorism' in the international community? Since 9/11 and the start of the so called war on terror, Pakistan has publically and consistently maintained that it will not allow its soil to be used for terrorist acts abroad. To the extent what was happening, whether through the Haqqani group or the Taliban using Pakistan as a sanctuary, the groups in question downplayed their use of Pakistani territory. And the Pakistani state suggested it was unable to seal a lengthy and porous border. What's changed now is primarily the international community's mood. Patience with Pakistan is running perilously low and the tolerance for errant behaviour may not be there.

Does it therefore make sense for Pakistan to flirt with attracting further international opprobrium in order to achieve the most limited of gains in terms of a short hiatus in violence inside the country? And by allowing TTP elements to once again push for closer ties with the Afghan Taliban, what happens when the 'goal' in Afghanistan is achieved? Would they not turn their sights back on Pakistan, stronger and more motivated than ever?

Pakistanis need to remember two things: one, the TTP has wrought great damage on Pakistan and will seek to do so again; two, an al-Qaeda-TTP combine would be devastating for the region.

TALIBAN'S LATEST MOVE COULD HELP PEACE DRIVE

The Taliban's latest move to open a political office abroad ahead of possible peace talks with the US could mark a significant step on the road towards a negotiated end to Afghanistan's bloody war. The Taliban announced recently that they had come to an 'initial agreement with relevant sides including the Arabian Gulf sheikhdom of Qatar' to set up their first representative office outside Afghanistan. This is a step back from the previous refusal to negotiate until all foreign troops have left Afghan soil.

If the move materializes, it could be a landmark in the search for peace after an eleven-year war waged by the Taliban against the government of Hamid Karzai and its US/NATO allies. The opening of an office would be 'good news for peace' but setback for Karzai as the Taliban would pursue direct talks with the US. It also shows that the Taliban are now under pressure and want to negotiate. Also, this means, that the Taliban are finally able to convince the US which is a big achievement for the Taliban and a setback for the government in Kabul.

The Karzai government, which had sought to drive any peace process itself within the country, has been outmanoeuvred by the Taliban with this move.[84] In the meantime, Karzai has agreed that if Washington wants to set up a Taliban address in Qatar to enable peace talks, he will not stand in the way as long as the talks are lead by his administration. But the possible shape of any negotiations is still elusive, as of the date of writing this essay, with the US government spokesperson refusing to respond to requests for reaction and the Taliban spokesman refusing to comment further or providing details. However the US government spokesman did reiterate that the Taliban reconciliation would only come on the condition of breaking from al-Qaeda, abandoning violence and abiding by the Afghan constitution. But, in a sign that the killing is unlikely to stop soon, despite 'talk about talks,' two suicide bombings killed some 15 people in the southern city of Kandahar the day the statement was issued.

There are still about 130,000 US-led forces fighting the Taliban-led insurgency across Afghanistan, with coalition combat troops set to leave the country by the end of 2014, handing control for security to Afghan forces. Both the US and NATO allies have been pressing for political solutions for an end to the war. The death toll of coalition service personnel in 2011 was 566 and includes at least 417 from the US and 45 from Britain, according to a tally based on figures from an independent website (www.icasualties.org.) the number is down from a wartime high of 711 in 2010 but up from 521 in 2009.

10

Attacks on the NATO Supply Line in Pakistan

After 9/11, when the US decided to attack and occupy Afghanistan, it realized the importance of Pakistan without which this mission would not succeed. Pakistan's President General Pervez Musharraf acquiesced and decided to join the US as an ally placing the country's airspace and the ground bases at their disposal.[86] An agreement was chalked out between the two countries whereby, besides cooperation in the military sector, Pakistan would provide a supply route for the US and NATO forces. The supplies would consist of fuel and other military equipment which would be transported from the country's seaport at Karachi to Afghanistan through the Khyber Pass or through Chaman in Pakistani Baluchistan. Afghanistan is a landlocked country and the access to a seaport is either through Iran or Pakistan. As the relations between Iran and the US were not good, the only alternative was Pakistan. It is also a historical fact, that even prior 9/11, supplies to Afghanistan were traditionally made through the Pakistani seaport of Karachi, for which a 'Transit Trade' agreement was already in place with the supply route clearly specified. This supply route is currently used by the NATO and US forces in Afghanistan.[80]

The supplies to the foreign troops through Pakistan began towards the end of 2002 and were made through the Chaman/Afghan, Torkham/ Afghan border and Nava Pass. The Chaman and the Nava Pass routes were rendered inactive by the militants within a few months, leaving the

Torkham route as the only viable option.[80] In the beginning, supplies were also made by air from Karachi and other airports in the country but the quantum was small. Consequently it was decided that to protect the land route, trucking terminals would be set up at different locations in the Peshawar City. The locations selected for this purpose were, Bara road, Kohat road and Ring road. A total of ten terminals were set up with names like Bilal, Al Feisal, Venus, Al Falah, and World Food Supplies and Logistics terminal plus others. These terminals were completed in 2006 and a private security company was hired to protect them. This was a mistake as the security company was unable or incapable of providing adequate protection. Between beginning December 2008 and 14 January 2009 over 350 fuel trucks, containers and other supplies were destroyed by the militants and 20 individuals also lost their lives. This was the beginning of a new blame game and finger pointing at Pakistan.

After 2008-09 the supply route came under repeated attacks by the militants. In January 2008, after repeated protests by the NATO forces, the Pakistan army launched an operation against the militants and criminal gangs in the Khyber agency and arrested 126 individuals. Nevertheless, attacks by the militants continued. All these attacks emanated from Peshawar and the Khyber agency.

Just a short distance from these terminals, at a point where the Bara district begins, the writ of the provincial government ends. All attacks on the NATO supply convoys also originate here. Again a few miles out of Peshawar, the convoy enters the Khyber agency. While the terminals can be protected, there is no security outside for the convoys, each of which usually consists of over 700 fuel and container laden trucks. These trucks are owned by local transport contractors who routinely pay the militants to protect their assets. Sometimes the deals would go awry and the militants would attack the convoys inflicting heavy damage. One contract transporter from Bara said that he had invested Rs 8 million (approximately $90,000) for the purchase of a trailer and truck, for which he was making a monthly installment of Rs 80,000 ($900) per month. He had been using a trailer truck for supplying fuel to the NATO forces in Afghanistan. His truck was subjected to a rocket attack within the Khyber agency limits, despite the protection money he was paying to the militants. The truck was destroyed and the driver killed in the attack.

Many contract transporters pulled out of the supply arrangements under threats from the Taliban. Others stayed on despite the risk, as the business was lucrative. The transporters would prefer an alternate supply route but there is none. According to the Pakistani custom officials at Torkham/Afghan border, which is the only remaining entry point, the number of fuel and container trucks entering Afghanistan vary between 60 and 300 on a daily basis. These trucks then move on to Jalalabad or the Bagram airbase near Kabul. The supplies arriving by this route constitute 60 per cent to 70 per cent of the requirements of the foreign forces.

The NATO troops are dependent on this supply route for just about all their requirements ranging from military vehicles to water. The World Food and Logistics Terminal in Peshawar has been the conduit for supply of heavy military vehicles, Humvees, armoured cars, jeeps, rockets, army jackets and other goods. The other major products transported via this route are gasoline, other oil based products, motor vehicle spare parts, wheat, rice, meat, medicine, tents, uniforms, shoes, soft drinks and water. The transit trade and the supply to military forces in Afghanistan is source of substantial revenue for the Pakistan Government. Seeking an alternate route in Central Asia will not be an easy task for the US and NATO due costs, political and logistic considerations.

The Pakistan army has arrested over 100 individuals most of whom belong to the militant group Lashkar-e-Islam. This hopefully would give some pause to the attacks on the NATO supply convoys. Pakistan remains a lynch pin in just about all issues pertaining to this war. Throwing up one's hands in desperation and declaring Pakistan as an adversary will not solve the problems and can exacerbate them further. Most issues somehow have a Pakistan connection, but it is imperative that the solutions also have to be found here.

NATO Strike on Pakistani Military Posts

Unfortunately, the US and Pakistan are presently embroiled in a serious controversy over a NATO strike in the early hours of 26 November 2011, on two Pakistani check posts, in which 24 Pakistani soldiers were killed. On Friday 26 May 2011 the NATO commander in Afghanistan met the Pakistan army chief in Islamabad to discuss communication and coordination across the Pak–Afghan border. Less than 24 hours later, troops at a Pakistani border check post in Mehamand became targets of NATO fire. Twenty-four of them died. According to the Pakistan military, the incident appears to be deliberate and the deadliest of its kind. A similar strike in September 2010 took the lives of two soldiers and another in June 2008 killed 11.

The Pakistani administration's reaction seemed designed not just to handle the issue domestically but also to send a strong signal to the US that this matter is not to be taken lightly. There was a flurry of activity in Islamabad and Rawalpindi, with the prime minister placing phone calls to the leaders of the major political parties and rushing back to Islamabad to chair an emergency meeting of the cabinet's Defense Committee. General Kayani, the Pakistani Chief of Army staff, called a meeting of senior army officers and declared the incident unacceptable. Disapproval was conveyed in Washington, Brussels and NATO supply routes to Afghanistan were blocked.

Previously such incidents were described as the result of miscommunication or of mistakes that took place during hot pursuit of militants. And it is true that Mohmand is an area through which the militants do cross the border. But the fact that the attack was aimed at a military check post, and that a large group was targeted (there were reportedly about 40 soldiers at the post), makes any explanation tenuous.[83]

Coming at a time when US-Pakistan ties had barely begun to recover, if at all, the incident's timing is also unfortunate for that relationship. Secretary of State, Hillary Clinton's visit in October 2011, had begun to improve somewhat after the latest controversy over the Haqqani network, but this threatens to sour relations and derail cooperation. The Pak-Afghan border has become increasingly dangerous for both countries, with incursions taking place in both directions. The need is for more cooperation not less. But the mistrust that an incident like this can foster will do nothing to bring that about.

The air strike by the North Atlantic Treaty Organization (NATO) at the Pakistani military post at Salala, in the Mohmand Agency, on the Afghan-Pakistan border on a Friday night is destined to become a milestone in the chronicle of the Afghan war.

Within hours of the incident, Pakistan's relations with the US began nose-diving and it continues to plunge. NATO breached the "red line". What is absolutely stunning about the statement issued by Pakistan's Defense Committee of the Cabinet (DDC), which met at Islamabad under the chairmanship of Prime Minister Yousuf Gilani is that it did not bother to call for an inquiry by the US or NATO into the airstrike that resulted in the death of 28 Pakistani soldiers.

Exactly what happened in the fateful night of Friday—whether the NATO blundered into a mindless retaliatory (or pre-emptive) act or ventured into a calculated act of high provocation—will remain a mystery. Maybe it is no more important to know, since blood has been drawn and innocence lost, which now becomes the central point.[83]

At any rate, the DDC simply proceeded on the basis that this was a calculated air strike—and by no means an accidental occurrence. Again, the DDC statement implies that in the Pakistan military's estimation, the NATO attack emanated from a US decision. Pakistan lodged a strong protest at the NATO Headquarters in Brussels but that was more for purpose of 'record', while the 'operative' part is directed at Washington.[84]

The GHQ in Rawalpindi would have made the assessment within hours of the Salala incident that the US is directly culpable. The GHQ obviously advised the DDC accordingly and recommended the range of measures Pakistan should take by way of what Chief of Army Staff General Ashfaq Parvez Kiyani publicly called an "effective response."[84] The DDC took the following decisions: (a) to close NATO's transit routes through Pakistani territory with immediate effect; (b) to ask the US to vacate Shamsi airbase in Baluchistan within 15 days; (c) to "revisit and undertake a complete review "of all programs, activities and cooperative arrangements" with US, NATO and the International Security Assistance Force (ISAF), including in "diplomatic, political and intelligence" areas; (d) to announce shortly a whole range of further measures apropos Pakistan's future cooperation with US, NATO and ISAF and, no more doublespeak.

The response stops short of declaring the termination of Pakistan's participation in the US-led war in Afghanistan (which, incidentally, is the demand by Pakistani politician Imran Khan (who is considered to be close to the Pakistani military circles). In essence, however, Pakistan is within inches of doing that.[85] The closure of the US–NATO transit routes through Pakistan territory may not immediately affect the coalition forces in Afghanistan, as it has built up reserve stocks that could last several weeks. But the depletion of the reserves would cause anxiety if the Pakistani embargo is prolonged, which cannot be ruled out.

Therefore, the Pakistani move is going to affect the NATO operations in Afghanistan, since around half the supplies for US-NATO troops still go via Pakistan. An alternative for the US and NATO will be to rely more on the transit routes of the Northern Distribution Network (NDN). But the US and NATO's dependence on the NDN always carried a political price tag—Russia's cooperation. Moscow is agitated about the US regional policies. The NATO intervention in Libya caused friction, which deepened the Russian angst over the US's perceived lack of seriousness to regard it as equal partner and its cherry-picking or "selective partnership".[84]

Then, there are other specific issues that agitate Moscow: US's push for "regime change" in Syria, the US and NATO appearance in the Black Sea region, continued deployment of US missile defense system, and the push for US military bases in Afghanistan. In addition, Moscow has already begun circling wagons over the US "New Silk Road" initiative and its thrust into Central Asia.

The future of the US-Russia reset remains uncertain. Washington barely disguises its visceral dislike of the prospect of Vladimir Putin's return to the Kremlin following the presidential election in March next year. Short of bravado, the US and NATO should not brag that they have the NDN option up their sleeve in lieu of the Pakistani transit routes. The Pakistani military knows this too.[84]

Equally, the closure of the Shamsi airbase can hurt the US drone operations. Pakistan has so far turned a blind eye to the drone attacks, even conniving with them. Shamsi, despite the US's insistence that drone operations were conducted from bases in Afghanistan, surely had a significant role in terms of intelligence back-up and logistical support. By demanding that the US vacate Shamsi, Pakistan is possibly shifting its stance on the drone attacks; its doublespeak may be ending. Pakistan is "strengthening" its air defense on the Afghan-Pakistan border. Future US drone operations may have to be conducted factoring in the possibility that Pakistan might regard them as violations of its air space. The US is on slippery ground under international law and the United Nations Charter.

The big issue is how Pakistan proposes to continue with its cooperation with the US-NATO operations. Public opinion is leaning heavily towards dissociating with the US-led war.[84] The government's announcement on the course of relations with the US/NATO/ISAF can be expected as early as next week. The future of the war hangs by a thread. Unlike during previous phases of US-Pakistan tensions Washington lacks a "Pakistan hand" to constructively engage Islamabad. The late Richard Holbrooke, former special AfPak envoy, has become a distant memory and special representative Marc Grossman has not been able to step into his shoes.[87]

Admiral Mike Mullen has retired as chairman of the Joint Chiefs of Staff and is now a 'burnt-out case' embroiled in controversies with the Pakistani military. Central Intelligence Agency director David Petraeus isn't terribly popular in Islamabad after his stint leading the US Central Command, while his predecessor as spy chief and now Defense Secretary Leon Panetta always remained a distant figure.

US Secretary of State Hillary Clinton is a charming politician, but certainly not cut out for the role of networking with the Pakistani generals at the operational level. She could perhaps offer a healing touch once the bleeding wound is cleansed of dirt, stitched up and bandaged. And US President Barack Obama, of course, never cared to establish personal chemistry with a Pakistani leader, as he would with Indian Prime Minister Manmohan Singh.

Now, who could do that in Washington? The horrible truth is—no one. It is a shocking state of affairs for a superpower with over 100,000 troops deployed out there in the tangled mountains in Pakistan's vicinity. There has been a colossal breakdown of diplomacy at the political, military and intelligence level. Washington trusted former Pakistani ambassador Hussein Haqqani almost as its own special envoy to Islamabad, but he has been summarily replaced under strange circumstances—probably, for the very same reason. At the end of the day, an intriguing question keeps popping up: Can it be that Pakistan is simply not interested anymore in a dialogue with the Obama administration?[84]

The heart of the matter is that the Pakistani citadel has pulled back the bridges leading to it from across the surrounding crocodile-infested moat. This hunkering down is going to be Obama's key problem. Pakistan boycotted the Bonn Conference on 2 December 2011. This hunkering down should worry the US more than any Pakistani military response to the NATO strike. The US would know from the Iranian experience that it has no answer for the sort of strategic defiance that an unfriendly nation resolute in its will to resist can put up against an 'enemy' it genuinely considers 'satanic'.

The Pakistani military leadership is traditionally cautious and it is not going to give a military response to the US's provocation. (Indeed, the Taliban are always there to keep bleeding the US and NATO troops.) Washington may have seriously erred if the intention on the night of 26 November 2011 was to draw out the Pakistani military into a retaliatory mode and then to hit it with a sledgehammer and make it crawl on its knees pleading mercy. Things aren't going to work that way. The regional situation works in Pakistan's favour. The recent Istanbul conference (2 November 2011) showed up Russia, China, Pakistan and Iran sharing a platform of opposition to the US bases in Afghanistan in the post-2014 period.

The Obama administration's grandiose scheme to transform the 89-year period ahead as 'America's Pacific Century' makes Pakistan a hugely important partner for China. At the very minimum, Russia has stakes in encouraging Pakistan's strategic autonomy. So does Iran. None of these major regional powers wants the deployment of the US missile defense system in the Hindu Kush and Pakistan is bent on exorcising the region of the military presence of the US and its allies. That is also the real meaning of Pakistan's induction as a full member of the Shanghai Cooperation Organization, which is on the cards.[84]

11

AMERICA'S NEW AFGHAN POLICY

There is no doubt that the Pashtun areas of Afghanistan and the tribal belt in Pakistan are now a focus of world attention. This is because the interests of many countries clash here especially that of Iran, Russia, China and the US. The impact of the politics here is felt in Central Asia, South Asia and the oil rich nations of the Arab gulf as in the coming days this region will play a significant role in the transport of oil and gas out of the Central Asian countries into South Asia. In fact the basic agenda, behind the Soviet occupation of Afghanistan, was to seek access to the warm waters of the Arabian Sea. Left unchallenged by America, the Soviets next conquest, would have been Baluchistan and the port of Gwadar in Pakistan, which lies in close proximity to the Persian/Arabian Gulf. This port has the potential of becoming a terminus, for oil and gas from Central Asia piped out through Afghanistan.[86]

Today, these very areas, located along the potential route of the pipeline, have become the centres of turmoil and unrest. For example, one possible route of the pipeline is from Southern Afghanistan (where the Taliban have a hold on the Kandahar province), to Gwadar in Pakistani Baluchistan. This is the shortest possible route and probably the preferred option. Both Southern Afghanistan and Baluchistan are today simmering with discontent against their respective central governments. The next option is a pipeline from Kabul to Peshawar and then on to Karachi. This route is also problematical due to unrest in the Khyber agency and also this is comparatively a longer route. The third option is a pipeline from

Central Asia to run south to the Iranian port of Chahar Bagh.[80] This is the longest route and not likely to materialize, although the Iranians have already started mobilizing their resources in anticipation of a breakthrough. One factor which weighs heavily against this route is the political animosity between the US and Iran. It will be difficult for a Central Asian country wanting to export its hydrocarbons, to obtain loans from any International Finance Institution, for building the pipelines. India is a fast growing economy with a huge appetite for energy. Consequently, a way has to be found to deliver the natural gas from Central Asia to the Indian markets. A possible route is from Afghanistan to Wana, Dera Ismail Khan, Multan located in Pakistan to New Delhi.

If the transportation of hydrocarbons from Central Asia is seen in the context of the upheaval in the tribal belt, a number of mysteries come to the fore. The unrest is not entirely about establishing an 'Islamic Caliphate' or the imposition of Sharia. It appears to be driven by the intervention of certain external factors. The clues come from the kind of modern weaponry being used by the militants and the finances available to them. Pakistan and the ISI can be ruled out because they have been on the receiving end of attacks from the Taliban groups in the country.[80] Also the country is too impoverished and perennially short of funds to spare any substantial amount for the militants. So, if not Pakistan, then who?

The Taliban groups in Pakistan maintain a mercenary force which is paid generously for their services. Also their foreign accomplices, the Uzbek and Arab militants appear flush with money and the most modern weaponry. Where do they get their weapons and funds from? The speculation rife in the region points towards two countries—India and the United States, channeled through the CIA—the invisible government? But what would the US gain from supporting these militants and destabilizing the region as after all it is fighting a war against these very enemies? The answer, perhaps, is that the US, as the sole remaining super power, is in the process of forming a new world order, taking into account the shifting economic and military centres of influence in the world. The wars in Afghanistan and Iraq resulting in the ballooning national debt are reasons forcing it to back away from its role as the gendarme of the world. It is as such, working to establish strategic partnerships in the critical areas of the world, where they can monitor and protect America's interests. For example, in the Middle East it is Israel which is America's proxy, and in South and Central Asia, the US wants India to play that role.[80]

There were high expectations when Obama became President, that there would be meaningful changes in American policy especially in regard to the Muslim world. His African ancestry and a Muslim middle name was the basis of hope for many who felt that the time had come for a more equitable relationship. Unfortunately that did not happen and Obama continued on the same path in foreign policy as his predecessor George W. Bush. While he has declared his intentions to withdraw the US troops from Iraq (end 2012) and Afghanistan (2014), his policy decisions are influenced more by the demands of a stalling economy and a runaway debt crisis than any moral considerations. His troops meanwhile are making no real headway in Afghanistan and appear to be headed for the same fate as the previous occupiers of the country. His relations with Pakistan, the lynch pin in this war, have taken a nose dive as the military in that country has spurned all US aid, in retaliation for the humiliation it suffered as a result of the unilateral US raid on the Osama hideout in Abottabad. They have instead decided to go their own way declining to oblige the Americans by opening a front in North Waziristan. The US is presently facing the dilemma of possibly losing the support of Pakistan, a nuclear armed nation of 180 million, for the sake of Afghanistan. This is compounded by pressure from the American people to bring this war to an end, sooner than later. The year 2012 is also an election year and apart from addressing the unemployment issue the Obama administration is mindful of the fact that it has to show some progress to the public on the Afghan front. The following appears to be the likely strategy, the administration will pursue in the coming days:

(i) Increase pressure on Pakistan's civilian Government and the military to do more.

(ii) A close watch to be kept on Pakistan's intelligence agency, the ISI whose activities are suspect, especially since the raid in Abbottabad on 2 May 2012 in which Osama bin Laden was killed.

(iii) Increase in the strength of the Afghan army. The additional forces to be posted in Kandahar where the Taliban has a strong presence.

(iv) Start negotiations with the 'good' Taliban to seek a path of compromise and peace.

(v) Increase drone attacks in the tribal belt of Pakistan with its tacit approval.

President Obama has also delivered a strong message to Pakistan that if does not act against the militants, America will. He backed this with a raid in Abottabad on 2 May 2012 in which Osama bin Laden was killed. The raid soured relations between the two countries as the Pakistan army felt humiliated at being kept in the dark by the Americans. The US action and its refusal to trust the Pakistan Intelligence, in sharing plans for the raid, displayed total lack of trust and confidence between the two supposed allies. Since then, the fences are being mended but the trust is gone. However, the realization is beginning to set in, that the two countries still need each other—Pakistan to fight the scourge of terrorism, which is destroying the very fabric of the country, and for the US the danger of losing Pakistan to extremism and destabilizing the entire region. After all, Pakistan is a nation of 180 million people, which is almost two third the population of the entire Arab world, and it has over one hundred nuclear war heads which could have disastrous consequences if they fall in wrong hands. America also needs Pakistan as an intermediary in negotiations with Taliban and other Pashtun elements. Pakistan itself is home to over 30 million Pashtuns who will always have a say in Afghan affairs.[80]

DRONE ATTACKS

In the war against terror, the strategy which has elicited a lot of opposition from the militants as well as the Pakistani authorities is the drone attacks in its tribal belt. Despite the protests from Pakistan at various International forums, the attacks continue. In fact under President Barak Obama these attacks have further intensified dashing the hopes of many commentators that the Obama administration would be more considerate of Pakistan's sensitivities and may perhaps, stop the drone attacks altogether. Since these attacks began in 2004, according to a conservative estimate, over 1000 persons have been killed ending year 2010. Those killed to date include a dozen members of the al-Qaeda and a large number of foreign fighters (Uzbeks, Chechens and others). According to one estimate over 118 drone attacks have taken place until April 2010, which include, North and South Waziristan, Bannu, Mohmand, Kyhber, Kurrum, Orakzai and Bajaur agencies. In first two and a half months of the Obama administration alone, there were 12 attacks in which 165 persons lost their lives which included foreign fighters and 13 security personnel. The largest number of casualties took place in Damdola of the Bajaur agency in which a missile was targeted at a school in which 85 were killed including children.[89] This attack took place on 13 January 2005. The other areas in which drone attacks took place were: Mir Ali, Syedga, Warsak, Mohmend agency, Angorada, Bagar, Zehrinoor, Miranshah, Jan Khel, Datta Khel, FR Bannu, Makeen, Danda and Damdola (three attacks) and Bajaur agency deserve mention. In fact all seven tribal agencies have been attacked in which besides the Taliban and foreign fighters, a large numbers of local citizens were also killed. They paid the price for providing refuge to the Taliban fighters or were living in close proximity of the targets. In all these attacks there was no attempt by the Pakistan Air Force to shoot down these drones, leading to the speculation that there was perhaps a tacit understanding with the Pakistan authorities, who would play to the public gallery in opposing the drone attacks, but were equally keen on getting rid of these militants.

The American's target in these attacks, besides the foreign fighters, was Jalaluddin Haqqani, the leader of the Taliban in North Waziristan. The madrasa he ran at Miranshah in North Waziristan was attacked on 8 September 2008 with missiles fired from a drone.[80] Haqqani escaped but 21 people including children were killed. The Americans consider the drones as a vital part of their war strategy. The results have been a success story in which many al-Qaeda leaders holed up in the inaccessible terrain of Northern Waziristan were killed. The Taliban's modus operandi, following the attacks, has been to recover the bodies from the target area as quickly as possible and transfer them to their camps. This is done to prevent the identity of the commanders killed being discovered by the Pakistani and US authorities.

There have been rumours, that in one such drone attack in November 2008, the number two leader of al-Qaeda, Ayman al Zawaheri was injured. A few days later the US TV channel CNBC alleged that a team of doctors was sent by the ISI to Waziristan to treat Zawaheri.[80] The story was never followed up and remained a speculation. The drones have successfully disrupted the communication systems and the movements of the Taliban and other militant forces in the tribal belt. They have, however, become a 'poisoned chalice' for the rulers in Pakistan, as the drones are viewed by the general public as a surrender of the country's sovereignty.

The prime target for these drones has been North Waziristan. Until 2008, Southern Waziristan was spared the brunt of these attacks. The situation changed when Baitullah Mehsud the leader of the Pakistani Taliban (TTP) based in South Waziristan began targeting foreign diplomats and bombing Pakistani cities. In 2009, the drones were used to attack the madrasas, militant camps as well as hitting the Taliban leaders as they moved about in cars. The attacks netted the scalps of some very prominent al-Qaeda leaders. This caused havoc in the ranks of the militants, who with the support of the religious political parties orchestrated a campaign to stop them. The first US drone attack in the tribal belt took place on 18 June 2004, in which the Taliban commander Maulvi Nek Muhammad was killed. In the attack on 14 May 2005, Hashim al Yamani an Arab commander was killed and on 1 December 2005 in an attack at Mir Ali, in Northern Waziristan, the Egyptian born Commander Abu Hamza Rabia was killed and finally in the attack on a madrasa at Damadola, in the Bajaur agency, 86 people were killed, most of them children.[80] A second attack was also made at Damadola but there were no reports of casualties. In the 2006 attack in North Waziristan, Mohsin Musa Mutwalli Atwa was killed. He was involved in the bombing of the US embassy in Kenya. On 8 September 2008, about 4 kilometers from Miranshah in North Waziristan, the house of Maulvi Jalaluddin Haqqani was the target of a drone attack. The missile missed his house and hit a madrasa. While Haqqani escaped alive, over 20 persons lost their lives which included some girl students.

In summary the drones have proved very successful, from the US perspective. These attacks carried out with the tacit agreement of the Pakistanis, have served the Pakistani and the US interests well. Without putting the US boots on the ground and thus openly challenging Pakistan's sovereignty, the end purpose of both countries—to eliminate the leadership of al-Qaeda and the Taliban—in this inaccessible and difficult terrain has been achieved to a large extent. The area, in many ways, has become a laboratory in which the art of fighting future guerilla wars, in mountainous terrains, is being written. A large standing army, in such a situation, does not serve a meaningful purpose. It is also cost prohibitive. Wars today can be fought sitting continents away using robotic machines like the drones, equipped with an effective surveillance and a missile delivery system.

The future danger to civilization will come not from warring states but from groups of individuals driven by radical political or religious orientation with a capacity to inflict unacceptable damage to the states or societies they live in. For this reason one must conclude that innovation in technology, to fight a new kind of war, has become the need of the hour.

12

AFGHANISTAN AFTER 2014

Viewed through today's political telescope, Afghanistan's future appears as turbulent as its past and ominous for Pakistan.[86] Hope for peace in Afghanistan was aroused when President Barak Obama declared that US and NATO troops would be fully withdrawn from Afghanistan by 2014 and responsibility and security and governance transferred to the Afghan National Army and the Kabul government. Apart from being responsive to domestic American sentiment, withdrawal is sensible, since the principle US aim of destroying al-Qaeda 'Central' in Afghanistan has been largely achieved and the Taliban-Pashtun insurgency is unlikely to be suppressed militarily.[85]

The US Secretary of State accepted the natural corollary-negotiations with the Taliban. Some well-publicized initiatives were launched for this purpose. Pakistan offered its help and conveyed the Kayani peace plan. However, it soon became clear that at least some components of the US administration continued to believe that a political settlement could be militarily imposed on the Taliban. The consistently optimistic assessments of 'ground realities' given by American commanders were contradicted by almost every other observer, American and non-American. [85]

Unfortunately the militarists' case was massively reinforced by the raid to kill Osama bin Laden and the success of the sharply escalated drone strikes. Secretary Hillary Clinton declared that we will simultaneously 'fight, talk and build,' in Afghanistan. Until the NATO attack on 26

November 2011 the US was able to cajole Pakistan into continuing its cooperation with this unwinnable, contradictory strategy. It is obvious that the American plans to build a 400,000-strong Afghan army and install an effective government by 2014 are unrealistic and unsustainable. The US cannot achieve in two years what it has failed to do in ten. Nor is the US Congress likely to continue allocating over $20 billion annually to subsidize the Afghan government and army. Without money and without a political solution, it is likely that the Afghan army will splinter into rival ethnic militias and the Kabul government will simply disintegrate.[87]

It seems the US has doubts about its own publically propagated plans. It is pressing Karzai to accept a 'strategic partnership' which—contrary to Obama pledge—would allow the US to station an unidentified number of its troops for an undetermined period of time in Afghanistan after 2014 for 'training' and support to the Afghans. A permanent US military presence in Afghanistan will almost certainly mean there will be no real negotiations with the Taliban or other Afghan insurgents.

Since the US is unlikely to be able to suppress the insurgency with a smaller force than it has at present in Afghanistan, it will need to rely on the continued support from the Northern Alliance to sustain its presence. The rump American force would probably be stationed in protected bases, capable of punitive forays against the insurgents but unable to 'hold' much less 'build' in most the south and east Afghanistan. As in the past, most of the blame for the failure is likely to be transferred to Pakistan. Acrimony could escalate to actual conflict, as witnessed after the NATO attack.

For this reason, and because of the threat of possible US military intervention from Afghanistan against its nuclear and strategic capabilities, Pakistan is likely to oppose the permanent military presence in Afghanistan. Iran too must be concerned about possible US or Israeli strikes against its nuclear and military facilities and thus likely to be opposed to an indefinite US presence. The opposition of Afghanistan's two most important neighbours will render the continued military presence in Afghanistan extremely difficult to sustain.

Given its proclivity to use force, it is entirely unclear if the US genuinely desires a dialogue with the Taliban. More likely, to use General Petraueus' words, 'to whack them to the negotiating table.' And, so long as the Northern Alliance leaders and other warlords are confident of continued American dependence on them, they are unlikely to be amenable to any plan that Pakistan or others propose for a political settlement with the Taliban. It is only if and when they see the imminence of total American withdrawal from Afghanistan that the hard-liners in the Northern Alliance will become open to an accommodation with their Pashtun opponents.

Thus, it is not surprising that the Kayani peace plan—to start with a halt in mutual hostilities followed by dialogue and political accommodation—has not evoked active support from Washington or Kabul. Awaiting resolution of the policy contradictions in Washington, Pakistan has temporized so far: cooperating with a negative US strategy, while seeking to prevent the destruction of some friendly or non-hostile elements among the Afghan insurgents in Afghanistan post-2014. After the last NATO attacks on Pakistan's border posts, Islamabad will no doubt seek to align its policy with its own national interest. Apart from closure of the NATO supply lines and the Shamsi airbase, this implies that Pakistan would limit cooperation with the US and NATO strictly to areas and issues where this serves Pakistan's own tactical or strategic objectives. Hereon, Pakistan's main objective is likely to be full and earliest withdrawal of US-NATO forces from Afghanistan.

A major dilemma for Islamabad is how to preserve those among the Afghan insurgents presumed to be friendly to Pakistan and simultaneously suppress the Tehrik-e-Taliban Pakistan (TTP) with its anti-Pakistan agenda. The TTP, it is said, has been able to sustain its attacks on the Pakistani military from 'safe havens' from across the border in Afghanistan. Reportedly, there is evidence that it has received support from Indian and Afghan Intelligence. Given this background, are negotiations an option with the TTP? The consequences of previous attempts were disastrous. Pakistan must also accord priority to eliminating the Chinese Uighur rebels reportedly detected among the TTP.

Iran is the third vital factor in Afghanistan. Prior to the US military intervention, Iran was the lead sponsor of the Northern Alliance against the Taliban with Russia and India in a supporting role. Iran maintains its links with the Northern Alliance and with Karzai. There are reports it may also support some components of the insurgency. Iran can critically help or hinder peace settlement in Afghanistan.[87]

Given the emerging common threat they face from the US/NATO presence in Afghanistan, there is scope for cooperation between Islamabad and Tehran. In particular, each can press their respective 'friends' in Afghanistan towards mutual accommodation. A north-south power sharing agreement in Afghanistan, brokered by the two neighbours, can bring a semblance of peace to Afghanistan and create the conditions for the US to undertake a full, orderly and honorable exit. The diplomacy required to promote convergence between Pakistan and Iran, despite their past rivalry in Afghanistan, and to convince the US that it is in its best interest to live up to its public pledge of full withdrawal from Afghanistan, can be conducted by a power with sufficient influence in Washington, Islamabad and Tehran. The UN is now seen as an appendage of the West and cannot play this role.[86] The one power well placed to play this role of brokering peace in Afghanistan is China. In a China led process, Russia, Saudi Arabia and Turkey can play a supporting role to bring peace in Afghanistan and end America's longest war.

What can the United States Accept?

The original plan for a post-Taliban Afghanistan called for a rapid, transformational nation building. But such a vision no longer appears feasible, if it ever was. Many Americans are now skeptical that even a stable and acceptable outcome in Afghanistan is possible.[101] They believe that Afghanistan has never been administered effectively and is simply ungovernable. Much of today's public opposition to the war centre on the widespread fear that whatever the military outcome, there is no Afghan political end state that is both acceptable and achievable at a reasonable cost.

The Obama administration appears to share the public's skepticism about the viability of a strong, centralized, Western style government in Kabul. But it does not think such an ambitious outcome is necessary. As the former US Secretary of Defense Robert Gates observed in 2009, Afghanistan does not need to become a "Central Asian Valhalla". Yet a Central Asian Somalia would presumably not suffice. Success in Afghanistan will thus mean arriving at an intermediate end state, somewhere between ideal and intolerable. Without clear limits on acceptable outcomes, the US and NATO military campaign will be rudderless, as well any negotiation strategy with the Taliban.

In fact, there is a range of acceptable and achievable outcomes for Afghanistan. None is perfect, and all would require sacrifice. But it is a mistake to assume that Afghanistan is ungovernable or that any sacrifice would be wasted on the pursuit of an unachievable goal. Afghanistan's own history offers ample evidence of the kind of stable, decentralized governance that could meet today's demands without abandoning the country's current constitution. By learning from this history and from recent experience in Afghanistan and elsewhere, the United States can frame a workable definition of success in Afghanistan.

From the end of the second Anglo-Afghan War in 1880 to the coup of Muhammad Daud Khan in 1973, Afghanistan underwent a relatively stable and gradual period of state building.[11] Although the country was an absolute monarchy until 1964, Afghanistan's Amirs (kings), on the whole, needed the acquiescence of the population in order to govern. The central government lacked the strength and resources to exercise local control or provide public goods in many parts of the country. Instead, it ruled according to a series of bargains between the state and individual communities, exchanging relative autonomy for fealty and a modicum of order. Over time, as Kabul improved its capacity to offer services and to punish the transgressor, this balance shifted, and local autonomy gradually eroded. But whenever this process went too quickly—most notably in the 1920s, under Amanullah Khan,[60] and in the 1970s under the Soviet-backed Peoples Democratic Party—conflict in the periphery erupted and local power brokers challenged the central authority.

The Soviet invasion in 1979 led to a fundamental breakdown of centralized authority and legitimacy, which resulted in the diffusion of political, economic and military power across a number of ethnic and geographic groups. The era of dynastic control of the state by Pashtun elites is now over.[82] Although war, migration and the emergence of regional strongmen have destabilized Afghanistan, local communities remain a fundamental source of Afghan identity and a critical base of governance and accountability. This is especially clear in the case of the local jirga or shura (community council). Traditionally, the community council was a place to solve problems and negotiate over common goods and burdens, with its more prominent members serving as liaisons to the central government. These bodies may differ in their power and representation, but they are still found today in virtually every community. This traditional and local base of legitimacy offers a potential foundation for stable government in the future.

Washington of course, would prefer to see Afghanistan ruled in accordance to the will of the governed, its people prosperous, and the rights of its minorities and women respected. But the United States' two main security interests in Afghanistan that justify waging a war are much narrower: one, that terrorists who wish to strike the United States and its allies not use Afghanistan as their base, and two, that insurgent groups not use Afghan territory to destabilize its neighbours especially Pakistan.

There are many end states for Afghanistan, but only a few are compatible with these national security interests. Afghanistan could become a centralized democracy, a decentralized democracy, and a regulated mix of democratic and non-democratic territories, a partitioned collection of mini-states, anarchy, or a centralized dictatorship. The first and the last are unlikely, partition and anarchy are unacceptable. But centralized democracy and internal mixed sovereignty are both feasible and acceptable.

Since 2001, Hamid Karzai's government, with international support, has pursued the model of centralized democracy. At first envisaged in the 2001 Bonn agreement and then codified in the 2004 Afghan constitution, this approach places virtually all executive, legislative and judicial authority in the national government. It has created the most centralized states in the world, at least on paper. The president appoints every significant official in the executive branch, from provincial governors down to middle level functionaries serving at the sub-provincial level. Although there are provisions to elect provincial, district, municipal and village councils, only provincial council elections have been held thus far. Kabul holds all policy, budgetary and revenue generating authority. In March 2010, Karzai approved a new governance policy that devolves some local administrative and fiscal authority to appointed officials and provides modest auditing and budgetary powers to elected sub-national bodies. Still, the Afghan state retains a remarkably centralized blueprint.

Political figures close to Karzai pushed for such highly centralized government against the wishes of many non-Pashtun minorities. From 1919 to 1929, for example, Amanullah Khan[60] aspired to be Afghanistan's Kemal Ataturk, but his strategy ultimately led to serious upheaval, which ended his rule. The radical attempts at centralization under the Soviet-backed regimes that followed the 1978 coup helped spark the mujahideen resistance that led to years of civil war.

After the Taliban were removed from power, in 2001, strong Pashtun support, combined with fears of a return to civil war of the 1990s, created a majority in favour of a centralizing constitution. But Afghan central governments have never enjoyed the legitimacy required by such an organizing principle. The last 30 years of upheaval and radical devolution of political, economic and military authority have only made this problem worse. Put simply, the current model of Afghan governance is too radical a departure in a place where the central state has such limited legitimacy and capacity. To create a lasting peace that includes the country's main ethnic and sectarian groups—as well as elements of the insurgency—Afghanistan will require a more inclusive, flexible and decentralized political arrangement.

Power sharing would be easier under a decentralized democracy in which many responsibilities now held by Kabul would be delegated to the periphery. Some of these powers would surely include the authority to draft and enact budgets, to use traditional alternatives to centralized justice systems for some offences, to elect or approve important officials who are now appointed by Kabul and perhaps to collect local revenue and enforce local regulation.

Increasing local autonomy would make it easier to win over Afghans who distrust distant Kabul and would take advantage of a pre-existing base of legitimacy and identity at local level. The responsibility for foreign policy and internal security, however, would remain with the central government, which would prevent even the most autonomous territories from hosting international terrorist groups or supporting insurrection against the state.

A decentralized democracy along these lines should be an acceptable option for the United States. Its reliance on democracy and transparency is consistent with American values. Individual territories with the freedom to reflect local preferences may adopt social policies that many in the United States would see as regressive. But the opposite could also occur, with some places implementing more moderate laws than those favoured by a conservative centre. By promoting local acceptance of the central government, this option would remove much of the casus belli for the insurgency. And it would preserve a central state with the power and incentive to deny the use of Afghan soil for destabilizing Pakistan or planning attacks against the United States.

A decentralized democracy would comport with much of the post-

Cold War experience with state building elsewhere. A range of post-conflict states in Africa (Ethiopia and Sierra Leone), Europe, (Bosnia and Macedonia), the Middle East (Iraq and Lebanon) and Asia (East Timor and tentatively, Nepal) have used some combination of federalism and other forms of decentralized democratic power sharing. Although it is too early to make definitive claims of success, not one of these states has collapsed, relapsed into civil war, or hosted terrorists. And some such as Bosnia and Ethiopia have remained reasonably stable for over a decade. This is of course, no guarantee that decentralized democracy would work in Afghanistan. But its track record elsewhere and its better fit with the country's natural distribution of power suggests that it offers a reasonable chance of balancing interests and adjudicating disputes in Afghanistan also.

A decentralized democracy in Afghanistan would face three critical challenges. The first is the Taliban, who oppose democracy on principle and are likely to resist this approach as aggressively as they now resist centralized democracy. The second challenge is the limited administrative capacity of the Afghan state. Decentralization would distribute power among a larger number of officials; for a state such as Afghanistan, which has a limited pool of competent bureaucrats, this could exceed the country's present human capital and require a major expansion of training efforts. Third, the country's power brokers would likely resist such an option. A transparent electoral democracy would threaten their status, authority and ability to profit from corruption and abuse.

Yet decentralized democracy could actually offer some important counter-balances in each of these areas. Hard fighting will be required to marginalize the Taliban under any democratic system, decentralized or not. The odds of success are much higher however, when the population supports the government. Counter-insurgency can be described as a form of violent competition in governance; it is much easier to win when the form of government offered is closer to the natural preference of the governed. And if the Taliban come to see their military prospects as limited, a centralized system might entice some of the members to reconcile with the government in the hope of securing a meaningful local role in areas where their support is strongest.

It will not be easy to combat high-level corruption or to improve administrative capacity. But a transparent system in which locals make most decisions would allow Afghanistan's traditional community leaders to police the use of power and public funds. A faraway national ministry in Kabul is beyond the oversight of a village or district *shura*. In contrast, local councils can see how the officials are spending money and take issue with uses which they find objectionable.

Decentralization may also improve the Afghan government's basic competence by allowing local officials to focus on smaller, more local issues. For example, the most widely hailed development program in Afghanistan, in the last eight years, has been the National Solidarity Program, under which the central government provides grants to democratically elected community councils for local development projects. The NSP was designed at the national level but is administered locally. To date, it has been fiscally efficient and effective, reaching more than 20,000 villages.[101]

Although centralized democracy offers no easy guarantee of success, it has much better odds of success than a centralized model. But it would not come cheaply: The United States would have to wage a sustained counter-insurgency campaign, provide major administrative assistance to the Afghan government, and conduct vigorous anti-corruption measures.

Mixed sovereignty is an even more decentralized model. Much like decentralized democracy this approach would take many powers now held in Kabul and delegate them to the provincial or district level. But mixed sovereignty would go one step further, granting local authorities the additional powers to rule without transparency or elections if they so chose—as long as they did not cross three "red lines" imposed by the centre.

The first red line would forbid local authorities from allowing their territories to be used in ways that violated the foreign policy of the state—namely by hosting terrorist or insurgent camps. The second would bar local administration from infringing on the rights of neighbouring provinces or districts by, for example, seizing assets or diverting water resources. The third would prevent officials from engaging in large scale theft, narcotic trafficking or the exploitation of state-owned natural resources.

Beyond these limited restrictions, local authorities can run their localities they saw fit with the freedom to ignore the will of the governed or engage in moderate scale corruption. The central government in Kabul would retain control over foreign policy and the ability to make war and enforce narcotics, customs and mining laws and limited authority over interprovincial commerce. Under such an arrangement, sovereignty is mixed to a much greater degree than in other possible systems, with many—but not all—of the ordinary powers of sovereign government delegated to the provincial or district level.

The mixed-sovereignty model would signal a more serious break with the direction of Afghan state building as it was conceived in 2001 than would decentralize democracy. But, it would also be a partial acknowledgement of the de facto arrangements that have taken shape since 2001. Many of the governors and other local officials appointed by Karzai have ruled not by virtue of a local mandate from Kabul but rather through their own local security and economic power bases, which operate outside the law but with tacit acceptance by Kabul. In provinces such as Balkh (under Governor Ata Muhammad Noor) and Nangarhar (under Governor Gul Agha Sherazi), this has led to relative peace and a drastic reduction of poppy cultivation.[98] Such warlords have settled into a stable equilibrium in which they profit from the theft of customs duties and state property but maintain order and keep their predation within limits so as to avert a mutually costly crackdown by Kabul. In other areas, however, strongmen have caused instability. In Helmand, for example, several years of corrupt rule by Sher Muhammad Akhunzada alienated significant groups in the province and sent poppy cultivation soaring, fueling the insurgency. Even in Afghanistan's stable north, the rule of the warlords has led to ethnic violence and criminal excess. To ensure stability, mixed sovereignty cannot amount to partition under local strongmen who rule with impunity in private fiefdoms. Redline restrictions that forbid the sort of excesses that fuel insurgency are thus essential.

Mixed sovereignty has some important advantages: It is less dependent on the rapid development of state institutions and offers a closer fit with the realities of Afghanistan. Restricting the central government's involvement in local issues to a limited—but aggressively enforced—set of redlines could encourage the power brokers to moderate their excesses, which now drive many towards the Taliban. At the same time, a mixed sovereignty system would depend less on transparency and efficiency, thus requiring less international monitoring, oversight and assistance. Local autonomy would create incentives for Taliban members to participate in reconciliation negotiations, since a more purely democratic option would subject them to electoral sanction.

However mixed sovereignty also carries risks and disadvantages that make it less consistent with US interests than either centralized or decentralized democracy. First, the governors would be free to adopt regressive social policies and abuse human rights. This would represent a retreat from nearly nine years of US promises of democracy, the rule of law and basic rights of women and minorities with costs to innocent Afghans and the prestige of the United States.[101] Corruption would also be prevalent—indeed, for prospective governors, the opportunities for graft would be an essential part of the system's appeal. The Afghan government would have to control the scale and scope of this corruption, lest official acceptance of abuse renewed support for the insurgency. To prevent this, Kabul would have to rein in the worst of today's excesses—if mixed sovereignty is merely a gloss for the status quo, it will fail.

At the same time, the Afghan state would have to crack down on the narcotics trade, which if left unchecked could dwarf the revenues provided by foreign aid and make such aid less convincing incentive for compliance with the centre. The central government would have to strike a bargain with the country's power brokers, requiring them to refrain from large scale abuses in exchange for moderate local corruption and a share of foreign assistance. Even this kind of bargain, however, would be resisted by the country's strongmen, who have grown used to operating without restraint. Thus, mixed sovereignty would not free Kabul from the need to confront local power centres, and even this limited confrontation could be costly and difficult.

Under this style of governance, there would be a potential threat of instability as powerful governors periodically tested the waters to see what they could get away with. The central government would presumably need to carry out periodic enforcement actions, including violent ones.

Mixed sovereignty is thus not ideal, but it could be viable and meet US security requirements if Washington and Kabul were willing to fulfill their roles as limited but important enforcers. The model offers the central government two means of imposing the essential redlines. The first is the threat of punitive military action ordered by Kabul. This would require security forces that have the capability to inflict serious costs on violators. The other reinforcement mechanism is Kabul's control over foreign aid and its ability to direct aid to some provinces but not others.

Washington would not be powerless, either—it would retain its influence through the disbursement of foreign aid and its deep engagement with Afghan National Security Forces. In order to maintain Afghanistan's internal balance of power, the United States and its NATO allies would need to pay constant attention. Otherwise the country would slip into uncontrolled warlordism and civil war. A workable mixed-sovereignty model is not a recipe for Western disengagement: it would require not only continued aid flows but also sustained military and political engagement. Regionalism diplomacy would be particularly important. To prevent Afghanistan from becoming a magnet for foreign interference and a source of regional instability, the United States would have to ensure that the country was embedded in a regional security framework. Such a framework would facilitate aid flows and discourage intervention by Afghanistan's neighbours.

As with decentralized democracy, internal mixed-sovereignty has produced tolerable outcomes in the developing world. Afghanistan itself was governed under a similar model for much of the twentieth century: Muhammad Nadir Shah and his son Muhammad Zahir Shah ruled for five decades as nominally absolute monarchs,[56] but with limited state bureaucracy and a certain degree of autonomy for the periphery. The rule of law was generally administered locally, and some Pashtun tribes in the south and the east were exempted from military service. Nevertheless, a national army and a national police force remained ready to enforce a few key royal prerogatives. The government earned revenue not from internal taxation but from foreign aid (starting in the late 1950s), foreign trade, and the sale of natural gas to the Soviet Union (beginning in the 1960s). Over time, as the government's capacity and resources increased, it was able to extend its writ, trying criminals in state courts, regulating the prices of staple goods, and bringing community land under its authority.

There are also external parallels. After the end of the Nigerian civil war in 1970, Nigeria had a weak federal government and a strong regional system, in which individual governors were free to organize local administration as they wished. Even today, the country retains some traits of internal mixed sovereignty. States in the Muslim north have sharia law, whereas others have secular judicial systems. The central government intervenes selectively to support unrest, such as in the Delta region. Although there are signs that Nigeria may be deteriorating, for most of the last 40 years it has functioned tolerably.

Many other outcomes for Afghanistan are possible—but would fail to meet the core US security requirements. The country could, for example, split up in a form of either de facto or de jure partition. The most likely split would divide the Pashtun south from the largely Tajik, Uzbek and Hazara north and west. Such a result would come about if a reconciliation deal with the Taliban granted the group too much leeway in the country's south, its historical power base. Any outcome that leaves the Taliban relatively free to operate in the south could create safe havens for cross-border terrorism and insurgency, similar to the use of Iraqi Kurdistan by the Kurdistan Workers Party, or the PKK, or the use of Congolese border havens by HUTU guerillas. Partition would also set the stage for proxy battles and internal competition for control of Kabul and key border areas. If the Karzai government collapses, Afghanistan could break down into the kind of anarchy and atomized civil warfare of the 1990s. Such a state would resemble the one that was taken over by the Taliban in the 1990s, or present day Somalia where lawlessness has created an opening for al-Shahab, a violent al-Qaeda supported Islamist movement —with obvious consequences for US interests.

Lastly, Afghanistan could become a centralized dictatorship, although this is hard to imagine. A single strongman is unlikely to be able to consolidate power in post-Taliban Afghanistan, where political, military and economic might is dispersed among numerous power brokers. In this environment, any prospective dictator—whether pro or anti-Western— would find it very difficult to prevent the country from descending into civil war. A coup d'état or anti-democratic power grab (amending the constitution, for example to allow for president for life) is entirely possible but not likely to yield stability in its wake.

Afghanistan has been a failing experiment in centralized democracy, heading toward de facto partition, with Taliban control in some areas and unstable, ill-regulated strongman governance in many others. This trend can be reversed. But, clinging to the original, centralized model will not help. Centralized governance matches neither the real internal distribution of power in Afghanistan nor local notions of legitimacy. There can be no effective military solution if the original political goal is so badly misaligned with the country's social and political framework. To its credit, the Obama administration appears to have realized that centralized democracy is a bridge too far for Afghanistan. Current policy is moving towards decentralization—the question is how far this should go and whether the Afghan and US officials can manage the transition successfully.

The shift towards decentralization can work, although it is no panacea. A system of either centralized democracy or internal mixed sovereignty would have its drawbacks and each would involve sacrifice and risk. In Afghanistan—as in most places—the more optimal a system of governance is, the longer and harder the fight to get it. The question whether to strive for the preferable outcome of centralized democracy or to accept the less appealing alternative of internal mixed sovereignty will largely be determined by the efforts and sacrifices the United States and its partners are willing to undertake. Yet for all their drawbacks, either approach would meet core US national security requirements if properly implemented. And either model is more achievable than today's goal of centralized democracy.

Moreover, a decentralized democracy would not require the Afghan government to abandon or amend the existing constitution. The 2004 constitution is flexible enough to allow many powers to be devolved through legislation, as demonstrated somewhat by the new sub-national governance policy, which provides limited administration and budgetary authority to local officials. A mixed-sovereignty model would clash with the spirit and the letter of the 2004 constitution, but such a system would likely evolve on a de facto basis, averting the need for a new constitution in the near term.

Afghanistan is not ungovernable. There are feasible options for acceptable end states that would meet core US security interests and place the country on the path towards tolerable stability. The United States would have to step back from its ambitious but unrealistic project to create a strong, centralized Afghan state. If it does, than a range of power sharing models could balance the need of Afghanistan's internal factions and constituencies in ways that today's design cannot, while ensuring that Afghanistan does not again become a base for terrorists. In war, as in so many other things, the perfect can be the enemy of the good. The perfect is probably not achievable in Afghanistan—but acceptable can still be salvaged.

END NOTES

1. Ludwig W. Adamec, *Afghanistan 1900-1923*, University of California, Berkeley, C.A., 1967.
2. Ludwig W. Adamec, *Afghanistan's Foreign Affairs to the mid-Twentieth Century—Relations with USSR, Germany and Britain*, The University of Arizona Press, AZ.1974.
3. "Afghanistan at a Glance," Press Department Publications, Kabul, 1957.
4. Van A. Nostrand*Afghanistan Land in Transition*, Princeton, NJ, 1963.
5. "Afghanistan, Present and Past," Afghan Publicity Bureau, Kabul.1958.
6. "Afghan Progress in the Fourth Year of the Plan," Government of Afghanistan, Kabul, 1960.
7. Afghan Transport and Travel Service, "Afghanistan Ancient Land with Modern Ways," London, 1961.
8. N.D. Ahmed, *The Survival of Afghanistan*," Peoples Publishing House, Lahore, 1973.
9. Asian Conference on Industrialization, "Industrial Development— Asia and the Far East," Report of the Manila Conference, Published by ECAFE, Bangkok, 1965.
10. Aziz Abdul Hai "Second Five Year Plan" Ministry of Planning, Kabul, 1963.
11. H.W. Bellew, *Afghanistan and the Afghans*, Sang-e-Meel, Publications, Lahore, 1979.
12. H.W. Bellew, "Afghanistan—A Political Mission in 1857 (with an account of the country and people)," Sh. Mubarak Ali, Lahore, 1978.
13. H.W. Bellew, *The Races of Afghanistan*, Sang-e-Meel Publications, Lahore, 1979.
14. H.W. Bellew, *Journal of a Political Mission to Afghanistan in 1957*, Orient Research Center, Lahore, 1978.
15. C.E. Bosworth, *The Ghaznavids*, Edinburgh University Press, 1963.
16. *Cambridge History of India*, Volumes, I, III, IV, V and VI.1950
17. Olaf Caroe, *The Pathans*, Macmillan, New York, 1964.
18. E.H.S. Clarke, "Afghanistan and Nepal,' Imperial Gazetteer of India, Sang-e-Meel Publications, Lahore, 1979.
19. Cruit Bette, "The Land of the Afghans," American International School, Washington, D.C. 1967.
20. Abdul Aziz Danishyar, "The Afghanistan Republic Annual Report," The Department of Publicity for Afghanistan, Kabul.

21. Nancy Hatch Dupree, "The Road to Balkh," The Afghan Tourist Organization, Kabul, 1967.
22. Dupree Louis, *Afghanistan in the 1970s*, Praeger Publishers, London, 1970.
23. Mountstuart Elphinstone, *An Account of the Kingdom of Kabul* Oxford University Press, London, 1972.
24. Vincent Lt. Eyre, *The Military Operation at Kabul*, Qoumi Maktab, Peshawar. 1972.
25. Arnold Fletcher, *Afghanistan, Highway of Conquest*, Cornell and Oxford University Press,U.K 1965.
26. W.K F Tytler, 'A Study of Political Developments in Central Asia.' Oxford University Press, U.K., 1968.
27. Government of India, "The Third Afghan War—1919," University of Calcutta, 1926.
28. George Grasmuck and Adamuck Ludwig (Eds.) "Afghanistan: Some new approaches," Centre for Near Eastern and North African Studies, University of Michigan, 1969.
29. Vartan Gregorian, *The Emergence of Modern Afghanistan—Politics of Reforms and Modernization, 1880-1946*, Stanford University Press, California, 1969.
30. John C. Griffiths, *Afghanistan* (with a historical note by Sir Olaf Caroe, Paul Mall Press, London, 1967.
31. Anous Hamilton, *Afghanistan*, Heinemann, London, 1906.
32. Henry Havelock, *Narrative of the War in Afghanistan in 1838-39* (Two Volumes), Henry Colburn Publishers, London, 1840.
33. Edward Hunter, *The Past Present—A Year in Afghanistan*, Hodder Stroughton, London, 1958.
34. Information Bureau, Royal Afghan Embassy, London. 'Afghan Progress in the Fifth Year of the Plan;' Weatherly and Sons Publishers, London, 1961.
35. Paul Jones, *Afghanistan Venture*, San Antonio, Texas, 1956.
36. Sayyed Khalil, *The Kabul Times Annual*, Kabul Times Publishing Agency, Kabul, 1970.
37. M.M.S.M. Khan (Ed.), *The Life of Abdul Rahman, Amir of Afghanistan*, John Murray, London, 1900.
38. Peter King, *Afghanistan, Cockpit in Asia*, Taplinger, New York, 196739. ???????
39. M. Klimberg, 'Afghanistan; Austrian UNESCO Commission Report,' Vienna, December 1966.
40. A.P. Kohzad, *Men and Events*, Government Printing House, Kabul, 1966.
41. Pavel Luknitsky, *Soviet Tajikistan*, Foreign Languages Publishing House, Moscow, 1954.
42. Patrick Macrory, *Signal Catastrophe*, Hodder and Stoughton, London, 1966.
43. Dr. A.M. Manzar, *Red Clouds Over Afghanistan* Institute of Policy Studies, Islamabad, 1980.
44. Konishi Mastoshi, *Afghanistan. Crossroads of the Ages*, Ward Lock and Co. Ltd., London, 1969.
45. Charles Mason, *Narratives of Various Journeys in Baluchistan, Afghanistan and the Punjab*, Bentley, London, 1842.

46. Woosnam Mills, *The Pathan Revolts in North West India*, Sang-e-Meel Publications, Lahore, 1979.
47. G.N. Molesworth, *Afghanistan 1919* (an account of operation in the third Afghan War), Asia Publishing House, London, 1962.
48. Mouth Lai, *Life of Amir Dost Muhammad Khan of Kabul*, Longmans, London, 1846.
49. Muhammad Ali, *Afghanistan, Land of Glorious Past and Bright future*, Education Press, Kabul, 1968.
50. Muhmmad Ali, *A Cultural History of Afghanistan* Kabul, 1964.
51. Muhammad Ali *Afghanistan, War of Independence, 1919*, The Punjab Educational Press, Lahore, 1960.
52. James W. Spain, *The Pathan Border Law*, Mauten and Co., Hague, 1963.
53. *Statistical Pocket Book of Afghanistan*, Ministry of Planning, Kabul, 1972.
54. Survey of Progress, 1961-62, Ministry of Planning, Kabul, 1964.
55. Sir Percy Sykes, *A History of Afghanistan*, Macmillan, London, 1940.
56. G.P. Tate, *The Kingdom of Afghanistan*, Indus Publications, Karachi, 1973.
57. V.M. Tomsky *The Truth about Afghanistan*, Navoste Press, Agency Publication House, Moscow, 1980.
58. Mary Bradley Watkins, *Afghanistan, Land in Transition*, D. Van Nostrand Co., New York, 1963.
59. Donald N. Wilber, *Afghanistan*, New Haven Conn, 1956.
60. Roland Wild, *Amanullah— Ex King of Afghanistan*, Nisa Traders, Quetta, 1978.
61. Andrew Wilson, *North from Kabul*, George Allen and Unwin Ltd., London, 1961.
62. Nancy Hatch Wolfe, *An Historical Guide to Kabul*, The Afghanistan tourist organization, Kabul, 1966.
63. John Wood, *A Personal Narrative of a Journey to the Source of River Oxus by the Route of River Indus, Kabul and Badakshan*, John Murray, London, 1841.
64. As'ad Abukhalil, *Bin Laden, Islam and America's New War on Terrorism*,Seven Stories, New York, 2002.
65. Yonah Alexander and Michael S. Swetnam, *Usama bin Laden's al-Qaida: Profile of a Terrorist Network*, Ardsley, New York, Transnational Publishers, 2001.
66. Daniel Benjamin with Steven Simon, *The Age of Sacred Terror*,Random House, New York, 2002.
67. John K. Cooley, *Unholy Wars: Afghanistan, America and International Terrorism*,Pluto, London, 1999.
68. Jane Corbin, *Al-Qaeda: In Search of the Terror Network that Threatens the World*,Thunder's Mouth Press/Nation Books, New York, 2002.
69. Diego Cordovez and Selig Harrison, *Out of Afghanistan, The Inside Story of the Soviet Withdrawl*, Oxford University Press,U.K 1995.
70. Louis Dupree, *Afghanistan*, Princeton University Press 1980; Empire, Presidio Press, California, 1993.
71. Alexandre Bennigsen and Enders Wimbush, *Muslim National Communism in the Soviet Union*, University of Chicago Press, Chicago, 1979.
72. Bill Gertz, *Breakdown: How America's Intelligence Failures Led To September 11*, Regenery, Washington, DC, 2002.

73. Rohan Gunaratna, *Inside Al-Qaeda: Global Network of Terror,*Columbia University Press, New York, 2002.
74. D.J. Herda, *The Afghan Rebels: The War in Afghanistan,*Franklin Watts, Danbury, Connecticut, 1990.
75. *Inside 9-11: What Really Happened,* By the writers and editors of Der Spiegel, St. Martin's, New York, 2002.
76. Ahmed Rashid, *Taliban: Militant Islam, Oil and Fundamentalism in Central Asia,* Yale University Press, New Haven, 2001.
77. Bassam Tibi, *The Challenge of Fundamentalism, Political Islam and the New World Disorder,* University of California Press, Berkley, 1998.
78. Paul Wilkinson and Brian Jenkins, *Aviation Terrorism and Security,* Frank Cass, London, 1999.
79. Robin Wright, *Sacred Rage: The Wrath of Militant Islam,* Touchstone, New York.
80. Aqil Yusuf Zai, *Talabanization, Afghanistan to FATA, Swat and Pakistan,* Nigar Publishers, Lahore, 2009.
81. Barnett Rubin and Ahmad Rashid, "Pakistan, Afghanistan and the West," *Foreign Affairs* 87(6), 2011.
82. Thomas Barfield, "Afghanistan's Ethnic Puzzle," *Foreign Affairs* 90(5).
83. Ron Moreau, 'The End Game' *Newsweek,* 10 June 2011.
84. 'The Nato Attack *Dawn,* Karachi, Pakistan, 27 November 2011.
85. Munir Akram, ' Afghanistan After 2014' *Dawn,* Karachi, Pakistan, 2 December 2011.
86. S.V. Salahuddin, *Islam, Peace and Conflict,* Pentagon Press, New Delhi, India, 2008.
87. Irfan Husain, *Fatal Faultlines: Pakistan, Islam and the West 'Dawn' Karachi,* 8 December, 2011.
88. Christopher M. Andrew andVasili Mitrokhin, *The World Was Going Our Way: The KGB and the Battle for the Third World,* Basic Books, New York, p. 409.
89. "President of Hell: Hamid Karzai's battle to govern postwar, post-Taliban Afghanistan," *The Times,* November 2011.
90. "Flashback: When the Taliban took Kabul," BBC, Urdu language commentary, Setember 11, 2010.
91. "Endorses the Special Report condemning of the abduction from the United Nations premises of the former President of Afghanistan, Mr. Najibullah, and his brother and of their subsequent summary execution," United Nations Resolution 51/108 article 10.
92. Milton Viorst, *In the Shadow of the Prophet: The Struggle for the Soul of Islam,* Westview Press, N.Y 2001.
93. Piggot Peter, *Canada in Afghanistan: The War So Far,*Dundurn Press Ltd, Toronto, 2007.
94. Ashok Kapur, *Pakistan in Crisis,* Routledge, London, 1991, p. 242.
95. S.M. Burke, *Pakistan's Foreign Policy: A Historical Analysis,* Oxford University Press, Karachi, 1990.
96. Stephen Cohen, *The Pakistan Army,* The University of California Press,Berkley California U.S.A. 1985.

97. Master Hewitt Vernon, *The International Policies of South Asia*, Manchester University Press, U.K 1952.
98. Robert Draper, 'Opium in Afghanistan *National Geographic*, February 2011
99. Syed Irfan Ashraf, "TTP Losing its Clout," *Dawn*, Karachi, Pakistan, 1 January 2012.
100. Sardar Ahmed, "Taliban Seeking Peace," *Dawn*, Karachi, Pakistan, 5 January 2012.
101. Stephen Biddle, Alexander Thier and Christia, Fotini, "Defining Success in Afghanistan," *Foreign Affairs*, August 2010.

INDEX

Abdali, Ahmed Khan, 21
Admiral Mullen, 94
Afghan Communist Party, 53
Afghan National Security Forces, 171
Afghan-Anglo war, 26
Afghanistan after 2014, 161-74
  What can the United States accept?, 164
Afghanistan Today, 82-97
Afghanistan
  Al-Qaeda Training Camps in, 66
  Historical Perspective, 13-31
    Advent of Islam, 14
    Nationalist Uprisings, 16
    Decline, 18
    Iran's Dominance over, 19
    Relations with British India, 21
    First Anglo-Afghan War, 24
    Beginning of the 'Great Game', 27
    Second Anglo-Afghan War, 28
    Border Issues with Pakistan, 45
  in 20th Century, 32-55
  Soviet Invasion of, 56-73
Afghanistan's Ethnic Conundrum, 74-81
Afghan-Pakistan border, 90, 150
Alexander the Great, 13, 129
Ali, Amir, Sher, 28
al-Qaeda Military Committee, 62
al-Qaeda, 9-10, 57, 60-65, 67-70, 72, 82, 84, 89-91, 93-94, 104, 106, 108, 126-27, 139, 141, 146, 158, 160
America's New Afghan Policy, 155-60
  Drone Attacks, 158
America's Pacific Century, 154
Amin, Hafizullah, President, 51, 98
ancient Greek Baktra, 16
Anglo-Afghan War, 165
Anglo-Russian Convention, 34
ANP (Awami National Party), 109
Ansar ul Islam, 120
ANSF (Afghan National Security Force), 91
Ashoka, 14
Attacks on the NATO Supply Line in Pakistan, 147-54

Babar, General Naseerullah, 105
Baghdad based Umayad Caliph, 15
Bhutto, Benazir, 103, 105
Black Hawk helicopter, 62
Brahman Shahan Dynasty, 14
Buddhism, 14
Bureau of Services, 60
Bush, George W., 157

CARE International, 86
CENTCOM, 72
Central Asian Valhalla, 164
Chamberlain, Sir Neville, 30
Clinton, Bill, former US President, 66, 93-94
Clinton, Hillary, US Secretary of State, 92, 153, 161
cloak and dagger agreement, 34

Collins, Joseph, 88

Darul Aman, 52
Daud's Governance, 48
Davis, Sir Henry, 36
De Montpellier College, 41
Defense Committee of the Cabinet (DDC), 150
Durrani dynasty, 23
Durrani, Ahmad Shah, 75

East India Company, 26

FATA (Federally Administered Tribal Areas), 10, 115
  Militant Groups in, 117
  Groups of Taliban forces in, 121
  Issues in
    at a Glance, 134
    educational institutes in, 135
    historical perspective, 132-38
    literacy, 135
    opportunities for earning a livelihood in, 136
Foreign Militant Groups in Pakistan's Tribal Belt, 125
Forward Policy Plan, 29
Frontier Crimes Regulation (FCR), 115

Gates, Robert, former US Defense Secretary, 91, 164
General Zia-ul-Haq, 99, 100, 102, 103
Ghamdi, Allama Javed, 110
Ghauri, Allauddin, 16
Ghaznavi dynasty, 16
Gilani, Yousuf, Pakistani Prime Minister, 150
Great Game, 9

Helmand Valley, 43
Henry, Kevin, 88
Hindu Kush Mountains, 43
Holy Mosques of Mecca and Medina, 59
How Pakistan was Talibanized?, 98-113
  Mindset of the Pakistani Taliban, 110
  Role of the Media, 107
  Taliban and the Political Parties in Pakistan's Tribal Belt, 109
  Talban's Restrictions on Arts in Pakistan, 112

Indian sub-continent, 47
International Security Assistance Force (ISAF), 84, 151
Iranian-Russian alliance, 92
Islamic Caliphate, 156
Islamic Movement of Freedom (IMF), 127
Islamic Movement of Uzbekistan (IMU), 127

JI (Jamat-e-Islami), 109
Joint Surveillance and Target Attack Radar System, 70
JUI (Jamat-e-Ulema-e-Islam), 109

Karmal, Babrak, President, 52, 58
Karzai, Hamid, 9, 80-82, 89, 145, 166
Khan, Abdur Rahman, 31, 76
Khan, Amir Amanullah, 35, 37, 39, 76, 165, 166
Khan, Amir Habibullah, 32-34
Khan, Dost Muhammad, 23-27
Khan, Genghis, 17
Khan, Ghulam Haider, 25, 26
Khan, Mir Owais, 20
Khan, Sardar Daud, President, 41, 44, 50
Khan, Sardar Nasrullah, 35
Khan, Sher Ali, 26, 31
Khyber Pakhtunkhwa (KP), 114, 135
Khyber Pass, 14
King George VI, 34
Kissinger, Dr. Henry, 49
Kurdistan Workers Party, 173

Laden, Osama bin, 57, 59, 71, 92, 102, 108, 157
  killed, 9, 158
Lal Masjid, 124
Laskar-e-Islam (Khyber agency), 149, 109
Launching Attacks on American Assets, 61

Lord Curzon, 32, 33
Lord Lawrence's (British India's Viceroy), 27
Loya Jirga, 45, 48

Mahabharata, 110
Marhattas of India, 21
Mazar-e-Sharif, 59, 133
Middle East, 59
Militant Groups and their Leaders, 114-31
MMA (Mutahida Majlis-e-Amal), 112
    government, 113
Mongol atrocities, 17
Mr. Jinnah, 115
Muhammad Zai Dynasty, 23
Mujahideen heroes, 85
Musharraf, General Pevez, 124

National Bank of Afghanistan, 40
Nehru, Jawaharlal, 47
New York City, attacks against, 83
New York City's Times Square, 139
Nifad-e-Shariat Muhammdi, 105
non-NATO ally, 92
North Atlantic Treaty Organization (NATO), 10, 80, 82, 83, 90, 92, 95, 96, 121, 127, 131, 149, 150
    Strike on Pakistani Military Posts, 149
    troops, 74, 129
North West Frontier Province (NWFP), 100, 106, 112, 114
Northern Alliance, 84, 104
Northern Distribution Network (NDN), 152

Omar, Mullah, 63, 64, 78, 102, 130
Operation Enduring Freedom, 68
Opium as source of Funding, 129

Pak-Afghan border, 149-50
pakhtunistan controversy, 48
Pakistani Intelligence (ISI), 11, 59, 100, 104, 107, 159
Pakistan-US relationship, 95
Pak-US Marriage, 95
Panjsher valley, 59
Parcham, 44
Pasha, Mustafa Kemal, 38, 39
Pashtun dynasty, 75
PDPA, 76, 77
Peoples Democratic Party, 165
Perovski, General Count, 46
post 9/11, 128
post-Cold War, 167
post-conflict states in Africa, 168
post-Taliban Afghanistan, 173
pre-9/11 civil war, 96
President Carter, 56
President Dr. Najibullah, 53
President Zia-ul-Haq, 106
Prophet Muhammad, 44
PTI (Pakistan Tehrik-e-Insaf), 109

Qajjar King of Iran, 25
Qajjar, Muhammad Shah, 23
Queen Humaira, 42
Quranic Sharia Laws, 45

Radio Kabul, 50
Rawlinson, Sir Henry, 26, 29
Research Analysis Wing (RAW), 11
Rig Ved, 13
Royal Afghan Infantry School, 41
ruler Taiful Maluki, 15
Russia attacked Kiva in Uzbekistan, 46
Russian expansion, 27

Second Anglo-Sikh war, 25
Shah Zaman, 22
Shah, Amir Nadir, 39
Shah, King Muhammad Zahir, 47, 98, 129
Shah, Nadir, 20
Shah, Taimur, 21
Shah, Zahir, last Afghan King, 41
Shola Javed, 43
Singh, Manmohan, Prime Minister of India, 153
Siraj ul Akhbar, 32

Soviet invasion, 130, 165
Soviet Red Army, 53
Soviet Union, 44

Taimur dynasty, 18
Taliban, 10, 70, 72, 74, 82, 84, 102, 106, 114, 167
  Funding sources of, 127
  latest move could help Peace Drive, 145
  Losing its clout, 139-46
  movement, 78
  Revive again, 144
  The Holy Warriors, 57
Taraki, Noor Muhammad, President, 50
Tehrik-e-Taliban Islamic (TTI), 143
Tehrik-e-Taliban of Pakistan (TTP), 9, 117-28, 139-45, 163
the lame one, 18
The Tass, 51

UN Security Council, 10
United States (US), 12, 41, 63, 67, 71-72, 80, 84, 87-92, 166-67, 171-72
  forces, 62, 71-73, 82-83, 106, 135, 141, 147,
  Relations with Pakistan, 90
UNODC (United Nations Office for Drug Control), 130
US-Indian-Afghan alliance, 92
US-Pakistan ties, 150

Viceroy Lord Lytton, 29
Viceroy Lord Minto, 33

White House, 88, 99
William Crowley, the BBC correspondent in Kabul, 50
World War I, 34, 56, 90
World War II, 41, 47, 90

Yusuf, Muhammad, 26

Zawaheri, Ayman, 102